D1412305

CHRISTOPHER

The Story of Ottawa Senators Right Winger Chris Neil

RON PEGG

CHRISTOPHER
Copyright © 2018 by Ron Pegg

ISBN: 978-1-4866-1672-5

Word Alive Press
119 De Baets Street, Winnipeg, MB R2J 3R9
www.wordalivepress.ca

WORD ALIVE
—P R E S S—

Cataloguing in Publication may be obtained through Library and Archives Canada

This book is dedicated to Chris, his wife Cait, their three children—Hailey, Cole, and Finn—and to the memory of Chris's mother, Bonnie.

Contents

Special thanks to the following for their contributions to this book:
Chris and Cait Neil
Barry, Jason, Dan, and Jeff Neil
Cathy Pegg
Frank and Cathy Colton
Ruth Butler
Linda Caswell
Muriel Stewart
Sandra Batchelor
Rob and Kellie Reed

If you think you are beaten, you are
If you think that you dare not, you don't;
If you'd like to win, but you think you can't
It's almost certain you won't.
If you think you'll lose, you're lost
For out of the world we find
Success begins with a fellow's will
It's all in the state of mind.
If you think you are outclassed, you are
You've got to think high to rise,
You've got to be sure of yourself before
You can ever win a prize.
Life's battles don't always go
to the stronger or faster man,
But soon or late the man who wins
Is the man who thinks he can!
—Walter D. Wintle[1]

---

1 "Walter D. Wintle, Quotes," *GoodReads,* https://www.goodreads.com/quotes/1033193-if-you-think-you-are-beaten-you-are-if-you, accessed April 4, 2018.

Prelude

It was the Christmas season when three-year-old Christopher and the rest of the Neil family were at the Peggs' home for their annual shared Christmas meal and exchange of gifts. Chris, along with the Peggs' three-year-old daughter, Stacey, were both dressed in their Christmas best. The red-haired boy wore a suit complemented by a bow tie. Both mothers were very pleased with the appearance of their respective youngest child.

After the meal was finished, the exchange of gifts took place. Christopher and Stacey acted as Santa Claus. They were giving the gifts to each of their family members when a problem developed. Everyone had a gift except Christopher and Stacey, but there were no more gifts under the tree. The two three-year-olds looked at each other, broke into tears, and ran from the room.

Stacey's dad's practical joke had not ended up as he'd expected. He'd removed the gifts and placed them in the closet to give everyone else a laugh. The tears were not supposed to be part of the joyful Christmas celebration.

It was seven years later, and again the two families were together to celebrate Christmas. Christopher was a Peewee hockey player playing on a team that was being coached by Stacey's dad. A hockey practice was scheduled for that evening. As a result, the coach and player had to leave for the arena just as the meal was finishing. As Chris was getting up to go, one of his brothers asked, "Chris, who is your coach?" Without hesitation, Christopher replied that his mother was his coach. His answer was no surprise to anyone. His mother was his coach.

It was a couple of years earlier when Miss Caswell was his teacher and John Mann his principal. She knew Christopher well, as Bonnie was her hairdresser. She was also with Bonnie and Christopher when they'd gone to Ottawa on Christopher's first visit to the capital. Miss Caswell was very aware that school was not one of the young redhead's favourite things. He usually had a difficult time concentrating on any school work. Mathematics was no different. Miss Caswell was trying to get him to learn some of the basic, important elements of math, but he wasn't co-operating. She spoke sternly to him. Christopher's response was that school was not important because he was going to be an NHL hockey player. He had also said something similar to his principal, Mr. Mann.

01
Family Roots

Both of Christopher's grandfathers, Hank Best and Dalton (Christopher's second name) Neil, were men whose lives featured a strong personality. Both made a major portion of their money by wheeling and dealing. One might call them horse traders.

Hank was a big man with powerful hands, similar to Christopher's hands. He was a rugged defenceman who never was afraid to get into a fight. He was his team's policeman. When Flesherton played Markdale, there was usually a fight involving Hank and Fred Peters. The two could be overheard before the game discussing who would instigate the fight that night. Close observers claim that you could see the smile on their faces while they were fighting. There was at least one occasion when Markdale and Flesherton were playing in Markdale that the Flesherton team left the arena by the window in their dressing room. The rivalry was very serious business. The fights were an important part of this hostility, yet there was the fun of it.

When Hank retired from playing, he coached the midget team that his future son-in-law, Barry Neil, played for. This, along with the school where Barry attended with Bonnie, was the beginning of the relationship between Christopher's parents.

Dalton Neil was not a hockey player. He did, however, take his two boys to the Rocklyn arena on Saturday morning for hockey. Dalton would spend his time in Rocklyn visiting and maybe working on a business deal. The boys would be on the ice at the little country arena for hours. During the week, the boys found patches of ice in the area of their home on the edge of Kimberley. They could be found hour after hour, day after day of each week, on the ice. When Barry got older and was playing organized hockey, Dalton did not show much interest.

Christopher's two grandmothers were highly respected women in their community. Velma Best and Wilda Neil both ran restaurants. The restaurant in Kimberley still exists as a restaurant today. The restaurant in Flesherton was just one of many business deals in which Hank got involved.

Christopher's dad, Barry, always loved to play hockey. In fact, in 2018—at seventy years of age—he still enjoys getting his skates on for a game of hockey. Like his father-in-law, Barry had the reputation of being his team's policeman. His exchanges with Keith Franks from the Dundalk team was regular news. The hockey exchanges were intensified by Keith's wife, Pat, and Christopher's mom, Bonnie, as both women have always had the deserved reputation of being extremely competitive and very strong willed.

On the ice, Barry never turned down the opportunity to fight. His elbows often led him to the penalty box. After the game was over, Barry could often be found sharing drink time and laughing with the same players he'd fought with during the game. Although Barry loves the game of hockey, his intensity for the game is as a player, not a spectator. When he's a spectator, he's much more interested in carrying on a conversation with a friend or an acquaintance than he is in watching the game.

On the other hand, Christopher's mother developed a passion for the game, probably as much from her father, Hank, as anyone else. She was, for sure, intense and competitive when Barry was playing. These characteristics of Bonnie continued to be very evident as she and Barry raised their four boys.

JEFF, DAD (BARRY) CHRIS, MOM (BONNIE), DAN, AND JASON

02
Bonnie, Christopher's Mother—and Coach

Bonnie loved her husband and her four boys with a passion. The word passion is the best word to describe Bonnie in all areas of her life. She loved Christmas shopping and would have all of her gifts bought long before the day. Then she'd see something else that she'd like to buy for someone. She'd forget all about the first present and buy the second gift. Her beautifully decorated Christmas tree would almost be suffocated by the gifts placed around it.

She also loved to entertain. Many times the hockey team would go to the Neils' after a game. This was particularly true of her husband's Flesherton Saints team. It almost goes without saying that if you entertain, you also enjoy cooking. The last great passion in her short life was opening a restaurant.

She certainly loved her boys, although she'd hoped Christopher would be a girl. As it happened, her best friend, Cathy Pegg, gave birth to a little girl, Stacey, a month before Christopher was born. Stacey became her little girl and, as a result, Christopher and Stacey grew up as best friends.

Bonnie's passion for life shone brightly in her love for sports. She developed a keen understanding of the game of hockey, even though she never actually played the game. In fact, she didn't believe that females should play hockey, and especially not on a men's team. During the era in which her boys played minor hockey, there were scarcely any women's teams. The only place girls could play a competitive game of hockey was on a boys' team. Bonnie believed that the female's position in sports was to be a cheerleader for the males. There's no question that her position on the subject would have changed today, considering that she has a number of granddaughters who are very good hockey players.

It was in the arena that her passions sometimes became unbridled. Cathy Pegg was very aware of this; although this best friend was also a passionate spectator, there was the occasion that an older friend of both of them, Dorie Weese, sat between them at a tournament game. Mrs. Weese stated that she would never make that mistake again, as she found herself being continuously elbowed on both sides.

During a game in Honeywood, Christopher's oldest brother, Jeff, was playing and got a penalty. The game was almost half over. It was observed that the coach's wife from Honeywood, who was also very passionate about her hockey, had moved to the side of the ice where the penalty box was. In fact, she was sitting right beside the penalty box. When Bonnie saw this, she took off around the rink … closely followed by Cathy, who was going to try and keep Bonnie out of trouble. They sat down right beside the wife of the Honeywood coach. No words were exchanged.

At the end of the period as the teams were leaving the ice, Bonnie and Cathy were returning to their normal seats. As they passed by the Honeywood coach, Bonnie stated to the coach that if he found his wife lying on the ice, he'd know who put her there.

It was a couple of years later that Dan, the Neil's second son, played with the Flesherton team that had won five consecutive Ontario championships in the E Division. Minor hockey allowed the Flesherton coach to reclassify the bantam team to A, as the previous season they had won the provincial championship final game ten to nothing. This team defeated Aurora, a much larger community, in the championship game of the Silver Stick in Midland with a late goal by the Peewee player playing with them, Kevin Sutter.

Aurora and Flesherton met again in the Ontario Minor Hockey quarter finals. Flesherton had won the first game in Aurora, and the second game was in Flesherton. The Aurora team and parents became very agitated that this little rural community was beating them again. Flesherton won their scrappy second game to take a two-game lead in the series. The Flesherton arena was packed. The Aurora team was inside the arena foyer on their way to their dressing room following the game when a scuffle broke out. The Flesherton coach quickly slammed the door closed to the foyer from the ice. The Flesherton team could not leave the ice.

Bonnie and Cathy were waiting close to mid-ice when Cathy saw the struggle taking place in the foyer. She thought to herself that she was glad she and Bonnie weren't in the foyer, but then realized that Bonnie was gone. She took off after her and caught up to her in the foyer just as Bonnie had turned and punched an older man, knocking him to the floor. She then said that she hoped that this was the person who pushed her. Her minister, Rev. Don Prince, had seen all the action. He assured Bonnie that he was. Flesherton won the series. The next night in Aurora, extra police were at the game. Aurora was down three players who had been involved in the foyer.

In reality, Bonnie's passion was always to look after her family and those who were close to her. Her reactions in the arena were above all else a concern for her family. This same passion could be seen when the Neils would annually host a Thanksgiving dinner. Amongst those who would be invited were her brother Bob and his wife Anne and their family, her sister Dean and her husband Milf and their family, the Ron and Eleanor Miller family, the Gwen Carter family, the Pegg family, and others from the Flesherton community and beyond.

03
Christopher's Early Years

LIFE WAS OFTEN RUGGED IN THE NEIL HOME, AND THE FOUR BROTHERS ARE each a product of their strong-willed parents. As is the case with many boys in a rural family, there were many exchanges between the sons. Christopher was the youngest, but he was often the instigator of the "small wars" which developed. On the other hand, Jason, the second youngest, enjoyed picking on Christopher, as he had been used as a punching bag by his two older brothers, Dan and Jeff. Regularly, Jason picked on Chris. The other redhead in the family, Daniel, would come to the rescue of Christopher. Jeff would then join in to support Jason. The fun had begun.

There was the normal day when a tent had been set up outside by the kitchen, and Christopher and Dan were playing in the tent. Jason decided it would be fun to take the pegs out that were holding up the tent, resulting in the tent collapsing on the two inside. As the tent collapsed amidst screaming and yelling, their mother came charging out of the house with her broom in hand. She was yelling that she was trying to do hair, as she ran a hairdressing business in their home. When the boys heard their mother coming, Jason ran to the barn, closely followed by Dan, who had escaped from the fallen tent. It was Christopher under the tent who took the beating from the broom. In all probability, Bonnie thought that Christopher, who is the child most like his mother, was the reason for the tent being in a heap.

Christopher and Bonnie were regular visitors to the Pegg home. When they were there, Christopher and Stacey often played with dolls. It was the time when every little person felt that they needed to have a Cabbage Patch doll. If you were to enter Stacey's room in the Pegg home today, you would find the room decorated as it was when Stacey went away to school over twenty years ago. On the top of the bed, amongst the pillows, sit two Cabbage Patch dolls. One of these belongs to Stacey. The other one is Christopher's.

The following day, the two would be playing at the Neil farm. They would be out in the barn above the hay mound, which often had very little hay in it, and the two of them would be walking across one of the beams near the top of the barn.

On another day, the twosome was in downtown Flesherton in Duncan's Home Hardware. Mothers' Day was coming, and Stacey saw a nice clock she thought her mother would like. But she had a problem—she had no money. Christopher stated that this was not a problem. She could just charge the clock to her mother and father's bill at the store. The only problem with this was that the Peggs didn't have a bill. However, Duncan's knew that this was no problem. It was called small town living in the 1980s. Stacey brought home the present of the clock for her mother. The bill was paid a few days later.

When the two of them took up square dancing with their friends from their class in school, Miss Caswell, along with the other leaders, thought it would be good for Christopher and Stacey to be partners. Christopher was far from being a graceful dancer. Miss Caswell felt that Stacey would be able to quietly work with her friend. This square dance group won a number of championship ribbons both at the local Dundalk competition and the Royal Winter Fair in Toronto.

CHRIS'S SQUARE DANCING GROUP

CHRIS'S FIRST TRIP TO OTTAWA

04
Christopher's Early Adventures in the Sports World

IT WAS ALWAYS AN INTERESTING EVENT WHEN CHRISTOPHER WAS THE BATTER the year that he began playing baseball. He would hit the ball for a single, but he never stopped running when he got to first. When the fielder threw the ball to second, Christopher just kept running. Because the ball was usually thrown off the base, he was headed for third. Eventually the ball would follow him to home plate. A single had become a home run.

It was a couple of years later that Bob Butler was his coach. Bob was coaching at third base. Christopher was on second. Mr. Butler had told him not to try to steal third base. It was a few seconds later. The other team had thrown the ball to third to get Christopher out as he was coming to the base. Bob Butler said to the redhead that he had told him not to steal. Christopher's reply was that he thought he could make it.

In his final year of Peewee baseball, Christopher's coach was Jamie Pegg. The team was playing in the Ontario championship game. Flesherton was losing. Coach Pegg sensed that the other team had completely run out of pitching. He instructed his players not to swing at any pitch until they had two strikes against them. The strategy was working well. Christopher came to bat. On the first pitch, he swung and hit a double. Coach Pegg quickly reminded the rest of the players that this hit was not part of the strategy. The other players understood that this was just Christopher. They continued to follow the coach's instructions. They won the game with walk after walk. They were the Ontario champions.

This same team had played earlier in the year in the Canadian National Exhibition Invitational Peewee tournament. Flesherton was, at this time, the second smallest community to ever play in this annual tournament. The town continuously played in the tournament for a decade. They had never won a game, but that didn't matter. The small-town boys were usually very competitive against the larger towns and cities. The entry fee for the tournament was free, and each of the players got a pass to spend the rest of the day and evening at the Exhibition. This year they played against Leaside from Toronto. The team did the impossible. They won! A key hit in the victory was a double hit by Christopher Neil.

And then there was hockey. Earlier in its history, Flesherton Minor Hockey had encouraged the development of the better younger players by having them play for the next-age-up team. As a result, Christopher's older brother, Dan, often got the chance of playing both on his team and the team a couple of years older when his team wasn't playing. This wasn't the policy when young Christopher came to play. As a result, he only got to play for his own team.

He was a defenceman, much like his father, Barry. Christopher was a good skater. He possessed a good shot. He always had skill in passing the puck, but his thoughts were more often centred on trying to score a goal rather than helping his little goaltender, Patrick Strutt, keep the puck out of his own net. Christopher and his good friend, Tim Goheen, who played forward, were usually the top two scorers on their team.

Christopher's home was now in behind the Flesherton pond. Many times he and Stacey Pegg would shovel off a part of the pond so that they could skate and play hockey; however, it wasn't unusual that the older boys would come home from school and take the clean ice for themselves. One time when his parents weren't at home, Christopher got all dressed in his hockey equipment and went out onto the pond. The ice was not thick. He fell through. His equipment became soaking wet. Christopher got out of the pond, took off the equipment, and put it in his equipment bag in the unheated garage. When he got to the dressing room at the arena for his next practice, he discovered that his equipment couldn't be worn, because it was frozen.

The young redhead always showed a love and concern for his fellow players. When Shawn Butler scored his fiftieth goal of the season, Christopher was quick to go to the goal and get the puck. When the referee said that they needed the puck to complete the game, Christopher gave him the puck but was quick to retrieve it when the game was over in order to give it to Shawn. This scene has been replayed on national television a number of times as Chris Neil has gotten the puck out of the net to give to a teammate on the Senators who has just scored a significant goal. The referee goes to the scorer's desk to get another puck.

Michael Stewart always gave his best as a member of this team. Michael was the smallest player. If some players from the opposite team tried to take advantage of Mike, Christopher was quick to be at Michael's side to give his support. Christopher's heart was always full of concern for his teammates. He was always their protector. In the language of pro hockey, this person is called an enforcer. In Christopher's case, he has a heart for his team and his teammates. He was and is much more than an enforcer. The welfare of his fellow players has always been a major part of this hockey player.

In Christopher's early years of playing, Grandpa Best would come into the dressing room after the game to give him a couple of dollars for each goal that he'd scored. After Christopher thanked Hank, Christopher would often remind the partially inebriated grandfather that it was his birthday. The loving grandad would then give Christopher an extra dollar or two for the ninth or tenth annual celebration of his birthday.

05
The Emerging Hockey Player

ALTHOUGH HIS HOCKEY TEAM IN FLESHERTON NEVER WON A PROVINCIAL championship, they were Ontario finalists and did win the regional Silver Stick to reach the North American championships. When Chris, which is what his teammates always knew him by, was playing Peewee, his coaches, Ron Goheen and Ron Pegg, discussed the possibility of moving him to the forward line and putting Tim Goheen back on defense. The change took place. Both ended up being drafted into the Ontario Junior A ranks playing their new positions. Although the move was for the betterment of both of these players, the move did not turn the team into a provincial championship team.

Bonnie was becoming restless about the future of Chris's hockey career if he remained in Flesherton. Flesherton Minor Hockey has always had the philosophy that it needs to do what is best for the player. Chris had a chance to go to Barrie and try out for one of their teams, and he went with Flesherton's complete blessing. He made the team, but then the OMHA (Ontario Minor Hockey Association) stepped in. They said that Chris couldn't play there, because it was out of the region where he lived. Unfortunately, no similar team existed near Flesherton. As a result, he had to return to Flesherton. It was only a short time after this that Ontario Minor Hockey completely changed this rule.

Chris was always a leading goal scorer and point-getter on his teams. In his last year of junior hockey in North Bay, he recorded seventy-two points in sixty-six games, which is better than a point a game; however, for the present time he was still in Flesherton, and he was entering his first year of Bantam hockey. The team didn't look like a very good team, even though it had as its coach one of the best coaches in minor hockey, Frank Colton. Bonnie and Frank discussed Chris's future. There was the opportunity to go to Durham, which had a much better team. Following their discussion, Frank reminded her of the Flesherton policy. Minor Hockey would not stand in Chris's way of going to Durham. He went.

When the Flesherton team list arrived on the desk of the local OMHA convenor, it was noticed that Chris Neil's name was not on the list. The convenor called Frank to ask where Neil was. Not wanting to get more deeply involved, the reply was that he didn't know. The convenor said that he would find him and send him back to Flesherton. The convenor followed through on his promise, giving Chris one day to get back to Flesherton or face suspension. The Flesherton Bantam team lived up to its promise. The season was not a good one.

That summer Chris had the chance to go to an elite hockey camp in Peterborough; however, one of those small-town mischievous events took place where a half dozen boys from Chris's age group were out for an evening of fun, which ended up with them "borrowing" a truck to get from one place to another. The young teenagers didn't realize that the owner, who had left the keys in the truck, was at home. They had just started to move the truck when the owner appeared. The boys all ran from the vehicle. Chris had only gone a few yards when he realized that the truck was in neutral on a slope. He stopped and went back to the truck to put it in gear. His decision to do this made it even easier for the owner of the truck to catch up to the boys. There were charges of mischief.

Bonnie was not happy with her son. She decided to not let him go to the camp in Peterborough; however, Jamie Pegg, who had played three years for the Petes and was highly respected by both Bonnie and Chris, talked with Bonnie and convinced her to let Chris attend the camp. This became his first major exposure to the management of junior hockey in Ontario.

As the fall season approached, Chris and his brother, Jason, went over to try out for the Junior C team in Mount Forest. The coach decided that he'd like Jason on his team, but he wasn't interested in Christopher. Jason, being Jason, spoke up and stated that if Chris wasn't on the team, he didn't want to be on the team. This was the end of Jason's junior hockey career. He has no regrets, as he and his wife, Tanya, work today with their two daughters, Taylor and Loren, who both are promising young hockey players.

The next season, Chris went to Orangeville to try out for the Junior B team. John French from Dundalk was part of the coaching staff. Both Chris and his good buddy, Tim Goheen, made the team. In Orangeville, Chris became a right winger, where he remained for the duration of his career.

French received word that North Bay was interested in his young right winger, but North Bay was concerned that the young redhead was maybe too soft to play on their team. John told Chris that the North Bay people were coming to see him play and what their concerns were. Chris got a Gordie Howe hat trick that night—a goal, an assist, and a major for fighting.

06
The Emerging Young Man

In the 1980s, Flesherton still had many of the characteristics of the typical small town in Ontario. These characteristics were beginning to disappear, but Chris developed into a young man living in this environment of a small rural village. He attended public school at the MacPhail Elementary school. When he was playing sports such as hockey and baseball, his teammates were the same guys and girls with whom he played on the school playground. His family attended St. John United Church, which was considered by most people to be the main church in the village. It was the church that the Reeve and the majority of the town councillors attended. It was the church where many of the teachers who taught at the village secondary school and at MacPhail also attended. The weekly attendance at church was at least one hundred people. Sunday school had over seventy children, and Vacation Bible School had over ninety children. Again, the same kids that Christopher went to school with and with whom he played sports were many of those same children who went to St. John.

The community was a close-knit group of people who shopped at the Flesherton Market, Avis's Drug Store, Kell's Dairy Bar (Jolleys), Colton's or Magees Gas Bar, and Duncan's Home Hardware. There was a security in just being part of the community. When Vacation Bible School was on, Chris often rode his bike from their farm to the church. He was always there. The beginnings of his faith had its roots in his young experience at St. John as well as from the faith of his mother.

Chris brought all of these small village experiences with him to Ottawa. He also brought with him his experiences as a businessman. With the assistance of his mother, he developed a grass cutting business, with customers not only in the village but in the surrounding rural area. One of his customers for most of that time was Mrs. Geraldine Robinson, who is known to have done more for the little village than anyone during the last decades of the 1900s. She was the major reason why the Grey Highland Secondary School was built in the village. Mrs. Robinson had nothing but compliments for her grass cutter. She always spoke highly of the young redhead, and she followed Chris's hockey career with keen interest for the rest of her life.

07
North Bay

CHRIS WAS GOING AWAY FROM HOME TO LIVE IN NORTH BAY WHERE HIS new team was situated. The North Bay franchise had a storied past, having been in St. Catharines as the Tee Pees when Rudy Pilous was their coach and where Bobby Hull, Stan Mikita, and Phil Esposito played junior hockey. When the team came to North Bay, the legendary Bert Templeton came with them from their latest home in Niagara Falls. Under Templeton, the Centennials had a number of exciting years, including winning the Ontario Junior Championship and playing in the Memorial Cup; however, the fortunes of the team were in decline following Mr. Templeton's decision to leave the franchise.

North Bay was the ideal place for Chris to continue his hockey career. It's a small city surrounded by acres and acres of rural countryside, and just over a three-hour drive from Flesherton. When Chris made the team, he was blest to be the first and only hockey billet that Bert and Mary Perrault ever billeted. He became an adopted son. Like Chris's mother, Marg was a great cook. When the first home game of the season was played, Barry and Bonnie were there. It was to be an exciting evening; however, the only time Christopher saw the ice that evening was when there were time outs.

The North Bay team continued the downward spin. By Christmas time, the decision had been made that the team would shed itself of many of its veteran players and go with its new recruits. Chris often found himself on the first line. He ended his first season with twenty-nine points in sixty-five games. He served 150 minutes in the penalty box. Chris's aim was to be a tough, rugged hockey player. He felt that he had the ability to be the next Darren McCarty. Darren was famous as a member of the Detroit Red Wings Grind Line that often played against the opposition team's top line. Darren was often an inspiration and the policeman for his team. He actually never served many minutes of penalty time, but he was well known for his willingness to fight the other teams' tough guys and inspiring his team.

Chris had been a good student of the basics of hockey. He was a good shooter but not a great skater. He was excellent in the corner. He had the ability to hit another player with a solid, clean body check. He knew how and where to pass a puck. Chris was never afraid to be in front of the other team's goal. He would give his best to screen the goalie and attempt to deflect the puck into the net.

In his second season in North Bay, this right winger amassed fifty-five points, including twenty-six goals. His time in the penalty box rose to 231 minutes. His family and friends from the Flesherton area continued to make regular trips to North Bay, especially for the Sunday home games. The road between the two centres can be quite wintry. On one trip, his brother Jeff drove his mother and her friend, Cathy, up to the game and home again. The trip home took all night, as they drove through a heavy snow storm. The people in the car often had their heads out the car window to see where they were going. They got home in time to go to work on Monday morning. It was an eight-hour journey.

The Centennials continued to improve, and in Chris's third year the team did make the playoffs ... although lasting just one round. Chris scored another twenty-six goals and had a total of seventy-two points in sixty-six games. His penalty minutes were once again just over two hundred. He was a well-rounded hockey player.

During the redhead's first two years in North Bay, his career was followed very closely by Marshall Johnston of the Ottawa Senators. In the spring before his last season in North Bay, Christopher Dalton Neil was drafted in the sixth round of the NHL player selections by Ottawa as the 161st player chosen.

08
Drafted in Pittsburgh

IT WAS A VERY EXCITED NEIL FAMILY THAT DROVE THE SIX-HOUR JOURNEY from Flesherton to Pittsburgh for the NHL draft. They'd been informed that Ottawa was very interested in Chris, and that some other teams were also showing some interest. When he was chosen by the Ottawa Senators and put on their team jersey, one of the people who greeted him and welcomed him to the team was Mike Fisher, who had been drafted in the second round. Chris had played against Mike, a member of the Sudbury Wolves, but had never met him.

Mike chose to stay around for the rest of the draft after he was chosen in order to meet all the players drafted by the Senators. No one would ever have guessed that this decision would be the beginning of one of the greatest chapters in the history of the Senators. The meeting of Chris and Mike was not only the beginning of a great chapter for the Senators, but it also was the beginning of an amazing friendship. Chris and Mike would return to North Bay and Sudbury for one more year before beginning their professional careers.

09
Striving to Play in Ottawa

WHEN NORTH BAY WAS ELIMINATED FROM THE PLAYOFFS FOLLOWING CHRIS'S third season, he was sent by Ottawa to the Muskegon Fury of the United Hockey League, which became the International Hockey League. The team had one regular season game left as they finished first in the league. Chris was in the lineup for all eighteen playoff games. The Fury won their first Colonial Cup as league champions.

The next season saw Chris playing with the Ottawa top farm club of that time, the Grand Rapid Griffins. During this season, he served 301 minutes in the penalty box as well as having a good season on offense.

He was invited to the Ottawa training camp. Chris had a good camp but was returned to the Griffins. Before Chris left for Grand Rapids, Trevor Timmins, a member of the Senators staff who served in many different capacities for the team for over a decade, took Chris aside to give him advice. The advice was that Chris needed to improve his grit game. If he was to make the Senators, Chris needed to get stronger and tougher. His future role with the Senators needed to be as the team policeman. The word enforcer was not the word used at this time.

The young redhead took the advice seriously. He worked hard at improving his strength and being the player that protected his fellow players. Chris came by the role of a protector very naturally. Part of the young hockey player's character was that he had become a team player who was very concerned for the welfare of his fellow players. As he was in North Bay, he became a great fan favourite in Grand Rapids. In fact, a couple of years after he moved on from Grand Rapids, there was a golf tournament and ball tournament in his home town of Flesherton advertised as a Chris Neil event. A number of his fans from Grand Rapids made the weekend trip to Canada to be part of this home-town celebration.

Following his second season in Grand Rapids, Chris once again was invited to the Senators' camp. Having followed the advice of Trevor Timmins, he was ready for the camp. His days in Grand Rapids were over. He was now a member of the Ottawa Senators.

10
The Enforcer

In 2016, Rob Del Mundo published a book entitled *Hockey's Enforcers—A Dying Breed*[2] in which he wrote forty-eight chapters on forty-eight different players whom he calls enforcers. The book includes players from as early as the 1920s, beginning with the great Eddie Shore. The word "enforcer" wasn't part of the hockey vocabulary in Shore's day. Such players were referred to as the team's tough guy. In all levels of adult hockey there has always been a tough guy needed to keep the opposing team in line. In many ways, the word "enforcer" doesn't describe the actual role that such players have had with their teams. Hockey, by its nature, is a game that requires grit and toughness. It requires a player who can get the attention of the other team.

It was back two decades ago that the amount of fighting in hockey games often dominated the game. It seems that fights were there for entertainment. It was also a way of attempting to attract new American fans to the game, as the American society appears to have a greater craving for violence than does the Canadian society. Most of this type of fighting has now gone from the game, which is a positive. However, the need for the tough guy on the team is very evident. Wayne Gretzky always had his policemen so that the other team couldn't take an unfair advantage of this skilled player. It's interesting that in 2018, Jim Rutherford, the general manager of the two-time defending Stanley Cup Pittsburgh Penguins, has been led to add a tough guy to be available to play with Sidney Crosby when the need arises. This is a result of last year's playoffs when the officials often didn't call a penalty on players who were actually illegally continuously hitting Crosby.

---

2   Rob Del Mundo, *Hockey's Enforcers—A Dying Breed* (Moydart Press, 2016).

Chris Neil is the second last player in the book of enforcers. The Detroit Red Wings' Darren McCarty also has a chapter written about him. Since Darren was one of the players that Chris felt he'd like to be similar to as a player, it's interesting to compare the two. The word "enforcer" doesn't even begin to describe what these two players contributed to their teams.

It's interesting that these two players' career goals and assists are quite comparable, even though McCarty played on a much superior Red Wings team that won four Stanley Cups during his playing days. McCarty also played over two hundred less games. Chris served more than a thousand more minutes in the penalty box ... but then again, the Ottawa winger played more games in the era of the fight of the night NHL than did McCarty.

Both Chris and Darren's lines would come onto the ice when the other team had all of the momentum. Their line would change the momentum right around. Their line would motivate their teams to playing much better hockey. Both players scored big goals or got important assists. Both were willing to get in the mix in front of the other team's net to help take the view of the puck away from the goaltender. Both were great corner men in digging the puck out and passing it to their player in front of the net. Both were tops in forechecking. Although Darren did develop some personal problems off the ice, both of these men have played significant roles in raising funds in the fight against cancer.

The more one studies the career of Christopher Dalton Neil, the more one comes to realize that this man, an NHL player in over one thousand games with one club (less than sixty players in the history of the NHL have achieved this), is much more than an enforcer.

Indeed, he is much more!

11
An Ottawa Senator

CHRIS'S DREAM OF BEING AN NHL PLAYER WAS NOW WITHIN REACH AFTER HIS very good second season in Grand Rapids. He had long since learned that you cannot take anything for granted. When the Senators held a ten-day development camp before training camp, he was there. It was his fourth development camp. It was possible that he could have taught the camp. It wasn't compulsory for him to be there, but he was.

He had become a believer in the lessons his mother had taught him when as a younger player he was out running in the summertime as a preparation for the next season. His mother would be right behind him in her car to make sure that he ran as far and at a pace that would keep him in top shape. His second oldest brother, Dan, had also pushed him. Dan was a six-foot-four power forward with exceptional hockey ability, but he never took the opportunity that was open to him.

When Chris arrived at training camp, he knew that the coaches already knew he could fight. He wanted to prove to them that he also could play hockey. Opposing players soon found Chris to be a pest that could not be shaken. In an exhibition game against Toronto in Orangeville late in the training camp, he scored a goal, got two assists, and manhandled the Leaf's Gary Roberts in a last-minute fight. He had his first Gordie Howe hat trick at the NHL level. At the time it was secondary that Toronto won the game five to four. Coach Jacques Martin stated that the line Chris played on was Ottawa's best in this game. Ken Warren of the Ottawa Citizen wrote that the young redhead was already a fan favourite.

Chris was continuously asked what had happened to his front teeth, which were missing. Most people anticipated hearing the details of a fight. With his typical big grin, Chris told them the story of playing summer hockey in Owen Sound. Somehow his stick got caught up in the goaltender's pads, which led to his mouth crashing against the crossbar of the net. The teeth were gone.

When the season began, young Neil was dressing every other game. The other player he was alternating with had compiled an excellent offensive record in Grand Rapids during the previous season. After a dozen games of this alternating, Chris had more goals and assists than the other player. He began playing every game. Chris scored his first regular season goal in Atlanta on October 31. It was the victory that allowed Ottawa to finish the month with a record of .500.

Chris's line had gained the title of the "crash and bang" line. Coach Martin encouraged the line to dump and chase. The three players would get the puck over the centre red line and then dump the puck into the corners of the other team's end. The three players were in hot pursuit of the puck. Their main purpose was to keep the puck deep in the end to create possible scoring chances and, if needed, to change the game's momentum in Ottawa's favour. Martin wanted the line to keep their game simple. Coach Martin was very pleased with their work ethic. He praised the threesome as the line continued to improve defensively.

12
Mike

CHRIS AND MIKE FISHER HAD MET ON THEIR DRAFT DAY IN PITTSBURGH. MIKE became a Senator in his first year out of junior hockey, and the two had the opportunity of getting to know each other better at the training camps before Mike's rookie year. By the time of Mike's second season, and Chris's second in Grand Rapids, the friendship had continued to blossom. They enjoyed each other's company.

When the redhead from Flesherton made the team the next season, Mike suggested that he'd be pleased to share accommodations with Chris. The Ottawa management thought it would be good for the two to room together when the team travelled. When Mike bought a rural home just outside of Stittsville, he invited Chris to live in the house, which was less than half an hour from where the Senators played.

Chris had developed solid roots in his Christian faith while growing up in Flesherton, yet he had seldom gone to church since leaving to go to North Bay. Mike grew up in a home in the Petersburg area where father and mother had deep Christian roots. Mike's Uncle David was the chaplain for the Toronto Blue Jays for twenty-nine seasons.

Laurie Boschman was an early captain of the Senators while playing in his final of fourteen years in the NHL. Upon his retirement, this young, Christian man became involved with Hockey Ministries International. He continued living in the Ottawa area. He began meeting with some of the Senators for a Bible study. Both Mike and Chris were often in attendance.

Interestingly enough, Mr. Boschman scored over five hundred points in his fourteen seasons, while spending over two thousand minutes in the penalty box. Laurie is only one of sixteen players to ever achieve this mark. He was a positive influence on the Senators, including the young redhead. During all of this time, the friendship between Mike and Chris continued to blossom. Along with the captain, Daniel Alfredsson, who had arrived in Ottawa a half dozen years before Chris, the three quickly became the face of the Senators. Alfie already was the face when the two younger players arrived. The two soon were almost as noticeable in the Ottawa area as Alfie. These three were the main ambassadors of the Ottawa team that was continuously improving year after year.

MIKE, CAIT, AND CHRIS AT CHRIS AND CAIT'S WEDDING

Letters from Ron

Mike Fisher of the Nashville Predators recently played his one thousandth game in the NHL. Less than 350 players have ever played more than one thousand games in the NHL. It is a major accomplishment and one that Mike can be rightfully proud of; it's even more of an accomplishment when one considers the rugged, hard-hitting brand of hockey that he plays.

A number of us in the Flesherton area came to know Mike through his friend, Chris Neil. Chris and Mike are very close friends. For a number of years, the two roomed on the road together while they both were members of the Ottawa Senators. Mike made a number of trips to Flesherton and participated in the Chris Neil golf tournament and other fundraising events to redevelop the arena after the big fire. He also spoke at the church service and gave his testimony at a breakfast in the Community Centre.

At one of these events, he and Chris signed autographs for over three hours. He was one of the players who flew from Ottawa to be part of Chris's mother's funeral following her fatal car accident. Mike's Uncle David has come to Flesherton on at least three different occasions to speak at church services during the many years that he served as the padre of the Toronto Blue Jays. Mike's mom and dad and his brother, Bud, have also made visits to the Neils and Flesherton. Bud played in the fundraising golf tournaments.

Mike was the honorary chairperson of the Roger's House, a home where small children who are dying from cancer may spend their last days. When Mike was traded to Nashville, Chris and Cait Neil became honorary chair of Roger's House, a capacity they are continuing to fulfill.

The trade to Nashville certainly showed that there are human beings in hockey that treat the players under them like human beings, and not just as a piece of meat at the market. Mike had married Carrie Underwood the previous summer. She needed to be in Nashville. Mike also needed to be in Nashville. Brian Murray, the recently retired General Manager of the Ottawa Senators, arranged a trade to take Mike to the Predators. There is no question that Mr. Murray would have preferred Mike to stay in Ottawa, but Mike needed to be in Nashville. It is a great human story. It is also a great story of God's provision.

Both Mike and Carrie continue to be ambassadors of the Kingdom of Jesus Christ.[3]

---

3   As appeared in *The Dundalk Herald, Flesherton Advance*, May 2016

13
Attending a Practice with Hanover Minor Hockey Team[4]

ONE THURSDAY NIGHT, CHRIS TOOK THE TIME TO ATTEND A MINOR HOCKEY team's practice when he visited the Hanover Boom's Canadiens Peewees. Joe Bak, assistant coach of the team, played minor hockey with Neil, and the two had remained friends. Bak invited Neil to come out to a practice during the NHL's Olympic break, and he'd agreed.

> "I'm pretty good friend with Joe," said Neil "We talk all the time and he's always talking about the team. I always hear a lot about them, so when you get the opportunity to come and meet them, it's something I wouldn't want to miss.
>
> "Whenever I was younger, I had people come out (to my practices) that I looked up to," continued Neil. "Whenever you can come out and help little kids that look up to you, it's a benefit for you as well."

Neil went through about an hour of drills with the team, focusing on the importance of good passing and communication. He also participated in a shootout with the goaltenders.

> "They picked (the drills) up really quick," said Neil. "The biggest thing is you have got to work on your passing. You have to be able to read the play well and know where the guys are— that's what I was trying to teach them."

---

4   Quotations in this chapter are taken from Dan Charuk, "Senator Practices with Hanover Team," *The Hanover Post*, February 19, 2002.

For the players, the opportunity to have an NHL player on the ice was very special. The kids were shy at first, but eventually they began warming up and talking to Neil.

"It was pretty fun," said Jeremy Hubbard. "He taught us a few drills. He's pretty quick. He's faster than us, bigger than us and he's a lot better than us."

"It was really fun," said goaltender Andrew Hughes. "It was a challenge. When he came in, he had moves, but by the time he got in close, he just shot, so it was pretty easy."

As fort facing an NHLer one-on-one, goalie Matt Lean said it was "no problem."

"I was just thinking, 'I've got to stop this,'" said Lean. "It was pretty cool, though. I never thought I'd get a chance to be that close to an NHL player."

It was the first time Kevin Edwards, coach of the Hanover boys, could remember an NHLer helping a local squad.

During the practice, Chris spoke with the local media about his rookie year.

"It's been unreal," said Neil, of playing in the NHL. "You think you've seen it all, and then the next night you find something else. You get to play against guys like Mario Lemieux and Steve Yzerman—it's just unreal.

"Game in and game out, you see guys that you're playing on the Sony PlayStation with. It's just overwhelming."

The highlight so far, he says, has been getting the chance to play against players he grew up watching, such as Lemieux.

"It was pretty exciting for me," said Neil. "I was kind of in a little scrum with (Lemieux) and I came up and he's like, 'Nothing here,' and I was like, 'Can I have your autograph?'"

The hardest part about being in the NHL, Neil says, is staying there. He says it is a struggle to stay on top of your game and play at such a high calibre every night.

"It's a big step (getting to the NHL)," he said. "Once you can get that, the speed is a little quicker and you got to have tape-to-tape passes all the time or the guys get mad at you."

Chris shared that he'd always hoped to make the NHL, and that perseverance is the biggest piece of advice he could give any minor hockey player with similar dreams: "Keep living our dream ... If you keep working hard, anything can come true. I had a dream when I was younger and I kept sticking with it."

Chris enjoyed his time with the local team and with the other teams the Senators help out with in and around Ottawa: "Whenever you can get out and do something like this for the younger kids, it's great."

14
Super Pest[5]

In a *Toronto Star* article published during the playoffs, Chris Neil was featured as a player who was unapologetic for his style of play.

> "I have to stay physical, whenever I can wear down their defence and tire them out. It's part of my job, I have to do what I do," Neil said here yesterday as the Senators prepared for Game 3 in this series tonight at the Corel Centre.

Even though Chris stayed out of the penalty box, he had a bone-crunching style and an ability to get under the opposition's skin that is reserved for the best "pests" in the game.

The Leafs claimed that Neil's hit on Jyrki Lumme in Game Two, which resulted in a concussion, was dirty. The Leafs didn't speak of revenge, but Lumme was placed on the long-term injury list and became the sixth Leaf regular with a genuine injury (joining Mats Sundin, Mikael Renberg, Dmitry Yushkevich, Garry Valk, Cory Cross).

> "It was a clean hit; it was just the way he was going," Neal said of the Lumme hit. "The refs even said it was a clean hit. I guess I caught him in the right spot ... The game goes on."

Leafs' coach Pat Quinn used the word "dirty" to describe the hit in his post-game press conference, but Chris didn't let that bother him. He liked the challenge of the playoffs: "That's just (Quinn) trying to stir the pot. He's using the media to stir things up."

---

5   Quotations in this chapter are taken from Mark Zwolinski, "Neil Among the Best of Pests," *Toronto Star*, May 6, 2002.

Chris had a run-in with a Toronto player earlier in the season when he threw a punch in a scrum that cut and blackened Gary Roberts' eye. After that, he became a regular on the fourth line and someone the Senators could call on when the going got rough.

Despite all this, Chris heeded Coach Jacques Martin's message about taking foolish penalties in the playoffs, even turning away from challenges from Donald Brashear and Tie Domi.

"It's tough—in the playoffs it's usually a close game and you don't want to put your team down or give the opposition some momentum," Neil said. "You can try to finish your checks and be a physical presence."

15
End of Chris's First Season[6]

CHRIS'S ROOKIE SEASON ENDED WITH A WIN BY THE TORONTO MAPLE LEAFS over the Senators. This was particularly frustrating for Chris, as Ottawa had two chances to end the series. In an interview after the game, he said:

> They've got a lot of guys with a lot of heart over there, but so do we," Neil said. "(Gary) Roberts was unbelievable for them and so was (Alyn) McCauley. We had a hard time shutting them down the whole series and they put us away ... We had a lot of penalties in the second so we had to be more disciplined and get more pucks on the net at (Curtis) Joseph ... You never know what can happen. We still had hope and we thought we could still come back and tie it up but that goal early (by Alexander Mogilny) put us down.

This particular game went into triple overtime before Toronto pulled out a three to two win. During each overtime intermission, the CBC showed Chris standing alone outside the Sens' dressing room, waiting for his teammates to emerge. It was something Chris had done all year; it was his way of getting focussed and pumping up the guys as they came out. He saw it as part of his role, trying to bring momentum to the team.

Over the course of his first year in the NHL, Chris compiled 231 penalty minutes, coming third in the NHL, but he wasn't a typical enforcer. He also scored ten goals, ranking tenth among NHL rookies, and saw a lot of time on the Sens' power play.

---

6 Quotations in this chapter are taken from Johnathon Jackson, "Neil Frustrated Over Senators' Loss," *Owen Sound Sun Times*, May 15, 2002.

If you had asked me at the start of the year if I would have had 10 goals, I probably would've laughed and given you a wink or something," said Neil, who will now become a restricted free agent but hopes to re-sign with Ottawa ... But I worked hard all year and the puck was bounding my way, I got a good opportunity and I went with it ... it was a good opportunity and I'd like to thank (the Sens) for that.

Chris followed the playoffs after Ottawa's elimination, cheering for the team that knocked his own squad out of the playoffs: "It'd be nice to see a Canadian team bring (the Cup) home, and I wish Toronto all the best of luck. Hopefully they bring it back to Canada."

16
Year Two in Ottawa

IT TOOK UNTIL THE MIDDLE OF SEPTEMBER BEFORE CHRIS AND HIS AGENT, Todd Reynolds, were able to come to an agreement with the Senators on a new contract. It was a three-year agreement that gave Chris an average salary of just under $700,000 a year.

In training camp, Chris broke a bone in his leg, causing him to miss the first twelve games of the season. When he returned, Chris was on a line with Mike Fisher and Peter Schaefer. Neil and Fisher often played together during the time that Martin was the Ottawa coach. The two complemented each other, as both were aggressive. In most games the two led the Senators in hits. Chris would not only lead the Senators in hits but would be the leader in the NHL. Both Chris and Mike had been taught how to check and do it legally. They kept their elbows and sticks down and led with their shoulder. As a result of their fierce forechecking, their line often kept the opposition bottled up deep in their own end. The line became a major reason why the Senators had long winning streaks. The team was in a battle for the top spot in the league.

Chris had learned that he must continuously strive to be disciplined and not take unnecessary penalties. On the other hand, he had to be ready to be aggressive when the occasion suddenly arose in the game. Chris was there to protect the skilled players. In a number of situations, Chris refused to be goaded into a retaliation penalty or a fight. As a result, the opposition player went to the penalty box. The Senators scored a number of important goals in the resulting manpower advantage.

Coach Martin stated that Chris was one of the team's most improved players, a result of his effort during his first season when he scored ten goals. Neil credited Mr. Martin with his increasing confidence. Martin was increasing Chris's ice time. Chris scored a number of his goals playing on the power play, where he became the man in front of the goalie making it extremely difficult for the goalie to see the puck. Martin stated that Neil is a smart player with a good set of hands. Although his skating had improved, he still needed to work on it. His understanding of the flow of play was good and would improve with more experience.

In mid-December, Chris went to the dentist with a tooth that was bothering him. The dentist decided that it wasn't a tooth issue but that Christopher had a broken jaw. He had been playing with the broken jaw for a month. As Chris said, had he known it was broken, he probably would have been out of action for at least a couple of weeks. After the diagnosis was made, the Ottawa tough man wore a mask to protect his jaw for the next number of games.

He never missed a game.

17
The Summer After the Season

THE SENATORS MADE GREAT STRIDES TOWARD BECOMING THE TOP TEAM IN the Eastern Division of the NHL. Coach Ken Hitchcock of the Philadelphia Flyers stated that Ottawa had the best right side in the league. He made this statement during the eastern semi-finals when Ottawa came from behind a two to nothing deficit in Game One of the series to beat Philadelphia four to one. Martin Havlet scored the first goal. Marian Hossa tied the score. Daniel Alfredsson scored the eventual winner. The three were the right wingers on the Senators' first three lines. Chris was the fourth line right winger. In Chris's own words, he raised the level of the right side of the team, and he did. His continuous hitting of the Flyers' defence forced them to play with their heads up. Chris was a continuous buzz saw. The Flyers were already down one of their top defensemen who had been injured in the previous round of the playoffs. When the season ended for the Senators, the team was already looking to the next season with anticipation of reaching an even higher finish than they had just achieved.

In the meantime, there was the summer. One of the significant happenings that year was the Chris Neil weekend in Flesherton in mid-July. He returned home to be part of a slo-pitch tournament and a ball hockey event where he played with the local youngsters. He was joined on the Saturday by Mike Fisher. The two of them signed autographs for over three hours! The signing took place while a beef barbeque dinner was being served to those who had bought tickets.

The weekend closed with an outdoor church praise service on Sunday morning. At the conclusion of the service, in typical Flesherton style, there was delicious homemade cake prepared and donated by one of

Chris's great fans, Bonnie Blackburn. Most of the money raised went toward the building of a new area hospital and to Flesherton Minor Hockey.

Chris also attended the Roger Nielsen hockey school outside of Lindsay for a second season. Roger Nielsen was no longer present at the camp, but he'd been at the camp the previous year and, in fact, every year of the camp's existence. Chris found it different, but the spirit of Roger was definitely there. It was pure pleasure for him to be able to assist the young instructors and spend some time with some of the campers. Chris recalled his own time at hockey camps and what it meant for him to see and get advice from a pro player. All ears and eyes were wide open to hear and see.

When he was home in Flesherton, Chris had taken time to spend a couple of hours in the hamlet of Priceville, where he visited the Vacation Bible School that St. Andrew's Church was holding. The school was under the direction of Gwen Kloosterboer, who had hoped that Chris might make an appearance. Over one hundred young children were present.

CHRIS EATING THE SPECIAL SALAD THAT HIS MOTHER ALWAYS MADE FOR HIM AT "CHRIS NEIL WEEKEND" IN FLESHERTON. THE SALAD WAS PREPARED BY RUTH BUTLER.

18
The Fall of 2003

IT WAS LATE IN NOVEMBER WHEN OTTAWA WAS PLAYING IN ATLANTA. THE team hadn't been playing well and had lost two games in a row. The opposition had scored the first goal in the game in all of the previous ten games that Ottawa had played.

The game had scarcely started when Atlanta scored the first goal. Captain Alfie could scarcely refrain from laughing, because the team had just received a pep talk before they went on the ice. The pep talk was to encourage them to score the first goal.

As the second period was winding down, Ottawa and Atlanta were in a tie game. One of the Atlanta defensemen cross checked Chris with the idea of getting Chris to retaliate. Chris did not. Neil had scarcely gone across the ice when the Atlanta tough guy tried to goad the Ottawa fighter into a fight. Chris did not respond. Atlanta was given two minor penalties, giving the Ottawa power play, which had the second-best scoring rate in the league, a two-man advantage.

As Chris skated by the Thrashers' bench, he smiled his toothless grin and then winked. The entire Atlanta bench came chirping at him. Chris was just doing his job. If the entire bench can be affected by what he has done, that is better than just one or two players. The coach could now set the offensively skilled players loose. Before the penalty time expired, defenseman Wade Redden scored his second goal of the game to give the Senators the lead and the eventual victory.

After another solid season came to a close with a first round defeat by the Maple Leafs, Coach Martin was relieved of duty and was replaced by Bryan Murray.

After Neil's first season under Martin when he scored ten goals, his production in the following seasons declined. The major reason that this happened was because the coach decided to use a different style of power play. Martin depended on skilled players to do the scoring. When the coach did want a body in front of the goalie, he was inclined to go with Chara, the giant-sized defenceman.

19
The Flesherton Arena

It was early in January of 2004 that a fire caused almost a million dollars damage to the arena where Chris had begun his hockey career. Much of the damage was caused by smoke. The arena wasn't able to be used for the rest of the hockey season. Flesherton showed its usual ability to respond to adversity. Using the nearby Markdale arena as its home, Flesherton teams came home with two Ontario championships.

It was in mid-April that a committee led by Rob Reed from minor hockey, Tom Gostick, the long-time arena manager, and Ron Pegg, a former arena board member and an original member of the minor hockey executive, approached the council with a plan to make changes to the arena. The entrance would now be at the side of the structure, an additional dressing room would be added, and the foyer of the arena would be more open. The estimated cost was $125,000. This wouldn't be covered by the insurance, which was going to be paying for the fire damage. The committee asked the council for a loan of the money, which the committee promised to repay within five years. The council was led by Mayor Brian Mullins and Deputy Mayor David Fawcett. The council was very cooperative.

The renovated structure was completed in late September. The loan was totally paid off in less than a year. One of the major reasons for this was the second Chris Neil Fan Appreciation event that took place in early August. The event raised over $30,000—one quarter of the money that had been loaned by the council.

The events of the weekend included a major golf tournament played at the nearby Highland Glen's course. A number of neighbouring community NHL players participated, including Jeff MacMillan from Durham and Aaron Downey from Honeywood. Mike Fisher, whom

Flesherton had come to adopt as one of their men, was a major participant along with his brother, Bud, in the events of the entire weekend.

A silent auction, which included many NHL jerseys that had been autographed and donated by various players, concluded at the banquet. The supper was able to be held on the floor of the arena while it was still under renovation. Fred Wallace from CFOS radio in Owen Sound was the evening's Master of Ceremonies.

The Saturday morning of the weekend had begun with an Athletes in Action breakfast in the Kinplex, next to the arena. This event was sold out, as a number of local people and local businesses sponsored tables of eight. Bob and Ruth Butler, two very avid fans of Chris, prepared most of the food. The two main spokespersons at the breakfast were Chris and Mike.

20
The Year of the Lockout

LIKE A NUMBER OF HIS TEAMMATES AND FELLOW NHL PLAYERS, CHRIS HAD the opportunity to sign a contract to play in Germany. The contract had a clause in it that would allow him to return to the NHL if the lockout ended; however, the Players Association and the NHL representatives didn't appear as if they were getting any closer to a deal. The season was a wipeout.

Chris turned down the chance to go to Germany. His reason was very straightforward: His father, Barry, was a strong union man. Chris believed that if he went to Germany, he'd be taking a job away from a player who would have been on the team. He couldn't go and take that job from that player. A good union person wouldn't do that to another person in their own profession.

Although the redhead spent time in Ottawa during this year, he spent even more time in his home town in Grey County. He got ice time in Owen Sound where there was some good recreational competition. In Flesherton, he could skate a couple of nights a week with recreational players, including members of the Neil family. He also joined a team in Flesherton's long-established, so-called Semi-Pro League. It was recreational hockey with a strong competitive spirit. The eight-team league had become a feature of the arena on Sunday mornings and Sunday afternoons, as Flesherton had a bylaw that didn't allow the minor teams to play in their home arena before 12:30 on a Sunday morning.

His three brothers and his father regularly played in this league. Chris was invited by the Durham Thundercats to attend some of their practices. The Thundercats had long been a team that graduates of Flesherton minor hockey went to play with. Durham is a short half hour drive from Flesherton. All three of his brothers had significant careers with the

Thundercats. Jeff, the oldest, held the record for the number of games played with the team. He also had the distinction of being the most penalized player in the team's history. Jeff was a fierce, aggressive fighter.

The Neil boys had all been important in the Thundercats' domination of the league for the biggest part of a decade. Dan Neil, along with Kevin Sutter and Jeremy Franks, all graduates of Flesherton, had been very important in leading the Hanover Barons to the Ontario Junior C championships before going to the senior Thundercats and being very important on their championship teams. Chris's youngest brother, Jason, quietly contributed to the champion teams.

Kevin Sutter was now the captain of the team. Another Flesherton grad and former Thundercat player, Rob Reed, was the coach. After Chris participated in a number of practices, it was suggested that he become a team member. Although other NHL players played senior hockey in Ontario, the WOAA league to which the Thundercats belonged stated that their laws and insurance wouldn't allow this.

In spite of the league's statement, the Durham management believed that there was nothing in writing to forbid Chris from playing. He joined the team for a game against Mildmay in Mildmay. The only problem that Mildmay had was that the Thundercats never let them know. They said that had they known, they could have advertised Chris, which would have led to a much larger crowd. Durham won the game. It didn't take long for the league to react. The win was taken away because Durham had used an ineligible player, and members of the coaching staff and executive received suspensions.

It wasn't long after this that Chris signed a contract with Binghampton, the Senators' American League team. He would join Jason Spezza for the team's last month and a half of the regular season and their playoff run.

21
A Silver Lining

THE YEAR OF THE LOCKOUT DID NOT END UP AS A GOOD HOCKEY EXPERIENCE for the great majority of NHL players. Chris Neil was one player who can agree with this statement. However, for Chris there was a silver lining. This is an understatement. It was not a silver lining—it was a platinum happening.

It happened at church. Chris was attending The Bridge, and a young lady whom he knew approached him after the service. Her name was Alyssa Doyle. She said that she wanted to introduce another friend of hers to Chris. The young, blonde-haired girl was Caitlin Sorensen.

Chris and Cait went to lunch at Jack Asters with a group of young people from the church. The conversation that began at the church carried on at the restaurant. They both found enough mutual interests to begin seeing each other.

When Chris was in Flesherton over Thanksgiving, driving in his car with his mother, his cell phone rang. Chris knew who was calling, He was excited and nervous. He ran over a curb while parking the car so that he could talk to this young university graduate. As a result of going over the curb, his mother hit her knee on the dash. She was not happy, but Christopher was.

It was only a few weeks after this that this young lady, the daughter of John and Sheryll Sorensen, came to Flesherton to the arena where Chris was playing in a "semi pro" hockey game. Cait spent most of her time at the rink not watching the hockey game, but instead talking with friends of Chris who were in the arena and were enjoying the new person in the redhead's life.

When in early March Chris went to Binghampton, Cait began making weekend trips to this New York city. The platinum lining was getting brighter and brighter.

22
A New Season

It was the fall of 2005. The redhead was very excited. He had met the love of his life, and he was looking forward to working with his new coach, Bryan Murray. Murray was excited, as he was finally, after a year of waiting, getting to coach his team. He believed that the young redhead would be an important part of this team.

It wasn't long before Chris was playing regularly on the power play. His willingness to crash the net led to him scoring a number of goals and causing havoc that led to other goals.

Early in November, Murray stated that Neil was working very hard and that Chris was getting a bit better with every game. All of this led to Chris gaining more and more confidence. It was also in this month that the Senators overtook Montreal for first place in their division.

Chris was playing on a line with Mike Fisher and Bryan Smolinski. The line was a force to be concerned about for the opposition. The unit never quit working. The line usually controlled the offensive corners of the ice; they were often the spark that ignited the team. During a game against the Sabres in Ottawa, with less than a second left in the first period, Neil scored the game's first goal. The goal was reviewed, and the review showed that the puck was in the net before the period ended. On the first shift of the second period, Ottawa scored again. This was followed by three more Senators' goals before the end of the period. That goal is a symbol of many of Neil's goals through the years. His goal or assist is often Ottawa's final goal of the game. It may also be a tying marker or the first marker scored in a comeback.

Through the years, the spark Christopher provided was more than a body check or a fight. In many ways, he continuously helped to provide the spark that got his team going. This spark included the much larger team of fans who would suddenly come to life to provide a seventh play-er for the team.

CHRIS, BOB CLARK, AND BOB'S GRANDSON CLARK

23
Tragedy

ON TUESDAY MORNING, NOVEMBER 22, CHRIS RECEIVED WORD THAT HIS mother had been killed that morning in a single-car crash on her way to Owen Sound to pick up supplies for the restaurant she'd recently opened. Her car hit a piece of black ice, and she wasn't wearing a seat belt. [Author's note: My wife says that if Bonnie were alive today, she still wouldn't be wearing a seat belt.] Chris immediately got a flight from Raleigh to Toronto.

The team was playing in Carolina that night. They won the game five to three with an empty-net goal. Coach Bryan Murray spoke to the team before they left the hotel for the arena. He said that the bus ride to the arena was the quietest bus ride he'd ever been on. The dressing room was quiet, and the players' bench that evening was very subdued. As Mike Fisher and Captain Alfie said, they wanted to win the game for Bonnie and Chris.

Mike knew Bonnie quite well, as he'd visited in the Neil home on many occasions. He said that Bonnie was very much like his own mother. Barry and Bonnie had been in Ottawa the previous weekend, as they made many trips to see Christopher play. Both Alfie and Mike said that the team wanted to win for Chris, because Chris always gave a hundred per cent for the team and for each player on the team.

On the Saturday of the funeral, eight members of the Senators' players and executive flew a charter to Owen Sound to attend the large tribute to Bonnie. They then returned to Ottawa for their game that night. A number of Chris's fans from Ottawa also journeyed to Flesherton.

As the author of this book writes this chapter, he's fighting tears in his eyes as he remembers the event over twelve years ago. He and his wife received the news while on a trip to Hawaii. They immediately flew home. They were joined by their three children who came from Phoenix, Calgary, and Los Angeles. Each of them, along with their mother, participated in Bonnie's memorial tribute.

Christopher was back in uniform in Ottawa on the Monday night. He said that his mother would want him to be there. Chris described the Ottawa dressing room as being a team of brothers. The team was very close-knit. The Senators were led at this time by an outstanding group of people who cared about others. Besides Coach Murray, the team was led by general manager John Muckler and the team president, Roy Mlaker and his wife.

During the remainder of the season, Barry Neil and those who travelled with him were always seated in the Ottawa team box. The Senators really were a highly loved and respected community team. This love and respect was also very evident in Chris's home town.

24
The Season Continues

THE OTTAWA SENATORS CONTINUED PLAYING OUTSTANDING HOCKEY, AND Chris was an important reason for the team's success. By February 13, he had twelve goals and fourteen assists. Four of his goals were scored on the power play. In total, Neil had eighty-five shots on goal. Each of these statistics were a season record high for Chris, even with a month and a half of the regular season to go. His fifth power play goal came when a Heatly shot hit him and was redirected by the hit so that the goalie was handcuffed on the play.

After Ottawa's thirty-first game of the season, the team had sold out twenty-seven of the games. By the end of March, the Senators had over one hundred points and became the first team to clinch a playoff spot. The team's record was forty-nine wins, sixteen losses, and seven ties. Chris finished the regular season with sixteen goals.

They were playing the Tampa Bay Lightning in the first round of the playoffs, the defending NHL champions. In the fourth game of the series, with Ottawa leading two games to one, Ottawa's top lines were not playing well. The fourth line of Vermette, Varada, and Neil had not been on the ice during the first thirteen minutes of the game.

When they hit the ice, they were flying. Chris said that it was very important to be ready to go when you had the opportunity. While on the bench, it's necessary to be glued to the game. The game requires the complete focus of the players. The line's shifts were to be just over thirty seconds. They were to go all out.

The line with Chris kept Tampa Bay hemmed in their own end. Grit players are extremely important in the playoffs. Although the grit line only played a little over seven minutes in a game that had many penalties, Vermette played over fifteen minutes because he was a penalty killer. This line was credited with keeping Ottawa in the game until the top lines got their game going. Chris scored his second playoff goal in the second minute of the third period. Ottawa then opened the floodgates for an easy victory. Ottawa went on to win the series, advancing to play Buffalo in the conference semifinals. Buffalo eliminated the Senators, putting an end to the Senators' exciting season.

Chris always showed his great love of the game. His smiling face around the arena was an outward expression of this joy for the game. He often said that within two weeks of ending a season, he was ready to go again. Early June found Chris already working out with plans of topping the past banner season; however, there was an even more important reason why Neil was excited. On July 8, his wedding with Caitlin was to take place.

25
Chris's Hands

A FIGHT MIGHT NOT LAST MUCH MORE THAN TWENTY SECONDS, BUT IT'S A fight with bare hands. It doesn't compare to a boxer who wears padded boxing gloves. It's bare knuckles against another person. It may even include a hit on the other fighter's helmet. At the very least, the hands may be required to remove the helmet of the other person in the fist fight. This means that the hands must be physically ready for slugging the other player. Chris puts new laces in his skates before every game. New laces, according to Chris, are easier to lace up than laces that have been worn in previous games. As a result, these new laces are easier on the hands.

The knuckles are the most important part of the hand for a fighter, as the knuckles take the main force of each punch. The better the fighter is, the more punches he throws. Chris is a fighter that punches with both hands. This meant that the knuckles on each hand got battered. The soreness of the hands from the last fight may mean that in tonight's game, the fighter isn't able to fight. His hands just won't take it. The shape that the hands are in can also affect the ability of the fighter to hold onto his stick.

There were practices in which Chris wasn't able to participate. His hand had bandages and cuts and bruises and were just too sore. Sometimes Chris would attend the practice and just skate in order to keep his legs game-ready. He would gingerly hold onto a stick while he skated.

Players who fight understand each other. They often talk to each other, as Chris's grandfather and Fred Peters did when they were preparing for a fight. The one fighter might say that he can't fight tonight, but the next time they play each other, he'll be ready to go. Chris usually wouldn't get into a fight situation with the player, as it could end up being a penalty for him without the other player getting a penalty. That would be bad on the part of Chris, because it would put his team in a man short, and the coach would not be happy. On the other hand, if Chris was forced into a fight situation when his hands weren't in any shape to fight, he was known to just take it for the team, leading to his team having the man advantage. During Chris's career, he spent 2, 525 minutes in the penalty box, which put him in twentieth place on the NHL's list of most penalized players in the history of the league.

Chris used the summertime to get his hands in shape for the next year. It usually took months before the hands felt good again. When the 2005 season ended, Chris was one of three players in the league to score over fifteen goals while spending over two hundred minutes in the penalty box. Obviously his hands were well managed by Chris and the Senators' training staff to be able to score sixteen goals, as well as being his team's protector.

26
A New Contract and a New Season

JUST BEFORE THE NEED FOR ARBITRATION FOR A NEW CONTRACT AROSE, NEIL signed a new three-year contract for over one million dollars a year. Chris was very happy that arbitration wasn't necessary, and he was overjoyed to be continually playing for the same team. He was pleased to be going back into the dressing room with his buddies and glad that he'd be able to be the first player to go out the door as the team headed to the ice for the start of a new game. When Chris went through the door, he'd wait to give each of the players resounding encouragement as they passed him by. He became the last player to go on the ice.

It was with great anticipation that he was preparing for the upcoming season with the desire to top his previous season. As the season progressed, coach Bryan Murray played him regularly on the third line. But if Murray felt the first and second line needed a wakeup call, Chris would begin the next game as the starting right winger on the first or second line.

Although Neil didn't always play on the power play, Murray would make sure that Chris was part of the unit if it hadn't been getting goals. He knew that Chris would go out and cause confusion in front of the opposition's net. This often led to the power play scoring a goal. Chris was scoring his share.

Neil's main function was playing with Mike Fisher. The two of them were leading the league in hits. In a game against New Jersey in late October, the Senators came out on top with an eight to one victory. Six different players scored for the Senators. Neil wasn't one of them, but he was named the first star of the game. Chris had registered a total of eleven hits in the game. Fisher was next on the list of hits, as he recorded four.

Murray's comment after the game was that Neil was rightfully the first star of the contest. On another occasion, Mr. Murray stated that

Chris Neil was the most improved player in Ottawa during the time that Murray had been with the team. Chris always said that part of his game was to hit any opposing jersey that got in his way or even close to being in his sight.

Neil believed that he had to continue to work hard. He had to get to the front of the net and he had to finish his checks. That's what got Chris into the NHL, and he had to continue doing this job if he wished to stay in the league.

By late November, Chris was leading the NHL, having recorded seventy-seven hits. Mike Fisher was behind him with seventy-one hits. The two were being called the Bash Brothers. Chris was usually the spokesperson for the two, and he continuously proclaimed that the two of them wanted the opposing defence to be very aware of when they were on the ice.

Neil continued to lead the league in hits. By the end of December, he had recorded 134 hits. Mike was third with 107. One of Chris's hits led to Chris Drury getting a concussion. Buffalo felt that Neil should have been suspended for the hit, but the league ruled otherwise. No penalty was called. Because of the Buffalo coach's reaction to this hit, the Senators' goalie, Emery, ended up in a fight. After Drury was injured, Ruff, the Buffalo coach, admittedly sent his tough guys out to hit the Ottawa skilled players. Emery, who was known to fight in junior hockey, didn't like Ruff's reaction. Following the game, Emery was reminded by the coaching staff to leave the fighting to the players who were supposed to fight when the event on the ice made fighting necessary. Emery also got a reminder from his mother that he should not be fighting.

Neil's reaction to Drury's injury was that he was sorry he got injured but hitting was a major part of his game. In his over one thousand games, Chris never received a suspension. By the time he completed his career, Chris had a record of 2,565 hits. This is fourth from the top for a player with the most hits in the league's history. His coach respected the redhead for his physical play but also the positive human being that he is.

27
The 2007 Playoffs Begin

It was the Pittsburgh Penguins in the first round of the playoffs. The Penguins had great promise but had not yet reached their potential. In game one of the series, Neil carried on as he had all year. He had led the NHL in hits with 288, thirty more than any other player. On a side note, Chris has said that the statisticians in other arenas don't always give credit for a hit. He cited one game in Columbus in which he had six good hits but was only credited with one.

During the year Chris had scored twelve goals, and three of them were game winners. He had often played on the second line but usually was on the third line. Murray continued to insert him on the power play. In game one against Pittsburgh, Chris scored a goal and got an assist as well as having three hits. Neil was a major part of the Senators' six to three victory. The Senators went on to win the series four games to one.

It was then on to Buffalo where the fans and the Sabres remembered Neil's hit on Chris Drury, even though Drury had stated that he had no problem with the check. There had been no penalty and no suspension. Chris expected the Sabres to target him. He had no problem with that, as hitting is very much a part of his game. He believed that if he wasn't hitting, he wasn't playing. Jason Spezza, a highly skilled player, believed that Chris was the Ottawa key to getting the Senators' rugged game going.

Chris expected to be loudly heckled by the Buffalo fans. Neil said that if the fans were not heckling him, he'd be worried. The heckling helps Chris get his competitive blood running at an even higher level.

When a couple of different reporters asked Christopher about his mom and her tragic death, Chris politely told them that he really didn't want to talk about his mother at the time. He needed to stay focused on the game and the series. At an earlier time, he had commented on just how important his mother was with her great love and knowledge of hockey. As a young teenager, Neil had over a dozen lawns to cut in the Flesherton area. When he had to be at a baseball or hockey game or practice, his mother would go out and cut lawns for him. She would not let this lawn cutting job interfere with the sporting events she believed were so important to his future.

As in the previous two series, the Senators defeated the Sabres four games to one. It was now off to Anaheim for the Stanley Cup finals. This was Ottawa's very first appearance in the final since they had entered the league in the modern era. The Anaheim team and fans did not have any firsthand knowledge about the Senators and Chris Neil. By the end of the first game in Anaheim, they knew what the hard-hitting Christopher was. He already had fifty-seven hits in his first fifteen playoff games.

Anaheim proved to be as hard hitting, if not more so, than Ottawa. After the first two games in Anaheim, the Senators were facing a new situation. The Senators were behind two games to none. The fans back home in Flesherton weren't daunted by this. Led by the local Kinsmen, a large screen was set up in the arena, and many in the community were in the renovated rink. There was great anticipation as the team returned to Ottawa for game three.

28
Hailey Jean Neil

CHRIS WAS NOT ONLY PLAYING IN HIS FIRST STANLEY CUP FINAL, BUT THE NIGHT before game three took place, he was at the hospital where his wife, Cait, delivered their first child, a little girl whom they named Hailey Jean. Jean was his mother, Bonnie's, second name. Chris was present in the delivery room to see the arrival of Hailey. Chris believed that he was being doubly blessed. He was in the Stanley Cup finals and he was honored to be present for the birth of their first child.

When the third game took place, Chris was credited with creating the Chris Neil hat trick. He had one goal, one assist, and "a baby." This was a play on the Gordie Howe hat trick (one goal, one assist, and a fight). Neil had stated that he wanted to score a goal for his new daughter. The determined Chris wanted to help his team and honour Hailey. He scored Ottawa's first goal of the game in the first period to tie the score. Ottawa went on to defeat the Ducks five to three.

When Chris entered the dressing room for the game, his excitement level was at an all-time high. Coach Murray stated that if there was one player who should start the game, it was Chris. His excitement level was a carryover from seeing the birth of his and Cait's baby. As Chris said, his wife did all the work. Describing the actual birth, Chris said it was unbelievable. "You can't say words to describe it. It's a miracle."

The result of the third game was encouraging, but the game was the end of the Stanley Cup dream. Ottawa lost the next two games. The team went into the record books as the Stanley Cup finalists.

29
Reflections

THE 2006–2007 SEASON WAS CHRIS NEIL'S SIXTH SEASON AS A REGULAR PART of the Senators. Over the course of the years, Chris had proven himself to be a top corner man. Defencemen throughout the league knew to keep their heads up when Chris was on the ice. His ability to hit the opposing players and then come up with the puck was part of his reputation. Having come up with the puck, he was very capable of giving a perfect pass to his fellow lineman in front of the net. Many of these passes didn't become goals, because at this time in the various players' careers they hadn't developed the ability to put the puck in the net. Most of these players never did become great scoring threats.

The major reason Neil's goal and assist record improved during the prior two seasons was that he was spending more time on the top two lines and was often on the power play. He was playing with players who had good offensive skills. Neil's ability to cause havoc and screen the other team's goaltender made him a valuable player on the power play. The shots from the point men often ended in the net. The late great Rocket Richard was as good as anyone in the history of the NHL from the blue line in. His ability to score important goals was in a class by itself. In a different way, Chris Neil had also become a great force from the blue line in.

Chris is the type of player whom you love if he's on your team; however, if you're from the opposition team, he's the type of player you're inclined to hate. His ability to throw clean hits on other players is one that many casual fans cannot understand. It's also an ability that many anti-Ottawa fans don't want to realize as part of his game. Chris came into the NHL with the ability to hit with his shoulders, not his elbows. He kept his stick down. As a result, his hit didn't have any element of a cross check. He didn't aim for the head, and he usually didn't depend on the boards to be part of his finished check, although a number of his penalty minutes were the result of hitting the opposition player too close to the boards. Although a number of opposition team fans felt that there were times that the redhead should get a suspension for his hit, the league officials never agreed with the anti-Neil crowd.

30
Changes in the Making

CHRIS AND CAIT WITH BABY HAILEY JEAN WERE MAKING THEIR HOME IN A newer subdivision area in Stittsville. The home was less than fifteen minutes from the arena. Chris is forever thankful for the time he lived in rural Stittsville on Mike Fisher's land. Chris holds dear his friendship with Tommy Genioli, another Christian friend of Mike's who came to live in Mike's home. Tommy came to Flesherton a number of times to help celebrate a Chris Neil event.

Marshall Johnston, the scout responsible for Chris being drafted by Ottawa, had long since moved on to other NHL teams. Roy Mlaker and his wife, who brought so much of a human touch to the Senators' organization, would soon be leaving. John Muckler, the general manager who had been the architect that brought together the Stanley Cup finalist team, was replaced by Bryan Murray, who had been brought to Ottawa to eventually be the GM.

The move of Murray from coach to GM was probably the most significant of all the changes happening for Chris. Bryan Murray showed his genius as a coach when he began using tough guy Neil on the power play and sometimes had him playing on the Senators' top two lines. The use of Neil in that capacity was one of the major reasons Ottawa reached the finals. Chris was one of the outstanding leaders on this team. He not only played well, but he was very healthy and played in all of the Ottawa games throughout the seasons that ended against Anaheim.

31
The Following Seasons

IT MAY HAVE BEEN THE BIGGEST PROBLEM THAT BRYAN MURRAY FACED AS general manager—replacing himself as coach. John Paddock, a long-time assistant coach, replaced Murray. The Senators started their season and were quickly on top of the league. However, this soon changed. The team was losing more games than they were winning. Murray showed very little patience with Paddock and fired him when the Senators still had a winning record. Murray took over once again, combining the job of general manager and head coach. This was a sign that the Senators would not get to the level of the Stanley Cup finalist team of the previous year. It was a beginning sign that Ottawa would never get back to this level during the remainder of Neil's career.

Chris was getting occasional time on the power play as the season moved along. Some of the sport writers wrote of Chris being important for his grit, but only as a fourth or possibly a third line player. A major knee injury forced Chris out of the lineup for over a month.

Ottawa lost its playoff round in four straight games to a Pittsburgh team that was rising to the top of the league.

The 2008–2009 season began with a new coach and many new players, as the Stanley Cup finalist team was experiencing major changes. Chris continued to be a major player in the community life of Ottawa. He represented the team at the Stittsville High School as the school launched a fundraising campaign to raise more money for school activities. This had been a program that the Senators had launched as a pilot project a couple of years earlier. Chris was greeted with a thunderous ovation as the students showed their love for Chris and the success of the program.

The Neils were building their new summer retreat north of Ottawa on the lake at Calabogie. Ken Zeggill, a friend and general contractor from Flesherton, built the beautiful, new summer home. Ken would come to Ottawa on Sunday night and work for the week on this project. Ken's helpers included Chris's younger brother, Jason, and a long-time friend of Chris's dad, Jim Davis. Chris's older brother, Dan, used his skills with a bulldozer to excavate the land.

The hockey season was a complete disaster, as Ottawa missed the playoffs. Chris was again hampered by the injury bug, and Murray once again fired his coaching choice in mid-season.

32
Would Chris be Traded?

THE SENATORS RETURNED TO THE PLAYOFFS IN 2010 IN THE SEVENTY-EIGHTH game of the season. They won that game over Carolina. The average attendance for the year was over eighteen thousand. Chris had his best season offensively since the Stanley Cup finalist season. He scored ten goals and had twelve assists. He spent just under two hundred minutes in the penalty box, adding to his team record as the all-time leader in that category. Neil also played in his five hundredth game as a Senator, becoming only the seventh player in franchise history to achieve this number of games.

Chris's love for Ottawa as a place to live continued to grow. When the February trade deadline of the NHL was approaching, his name was daily in the newspaper, as he was in the last year of his contract. His agent had been negotiating on his behalf, but what Neil was aiming for and what the Senators were offering were over 200,000 apart. The speculation was that if Murray couldn't sign him before the trade deadline, then he'd trade him. What the reporters were forgetting was Murray's love for the redhead kid from Flesherton. Murray did state that the trade deadline in 2010 was not a good market. Any offers that he received for Chris were far from acceptable.

The Senators played the defending Stanley Cup champion Pittsburgh Penguins in the first round of the playoffs. The Penguins won in six games. The fifth game was a game for the ages. Ottawa had jumped into an early three-goal lead, but the Penguins fought back to tie the score. The team played a modern-day record of three overtime periods before the Penguins won. No playoff game in the modern era of hockey had gone this long.

When the season ended, the Senators and Chris were still far apart in discussing a future contract. The day for free agency in July arrived. The Senators offer was for just over $1,800,000. Chris was asking $2,000,000. On the first day of free agency, Chris received two offers from other teams for over $2,000,000.

Chris personally met with Mr. Murray. He stated that he had these two offers but that he wanted to stay in Ottawa. He would sign with Ottawa for $2,000,000. It's important to remember the mutual respect Chris and Bryan held for each other. Murray stated that he needed to speak to the owner, Eugene Melnyk. He did. Christopher signed in Ottawa for four years for the sum of $2,000,000 a year.

33

An Exciting Year for Ottawa

ON ICE, THE OTTAWA SENATORS' 2010–2011 SEASON WAS NOT SUCCESSFUL. For the second time in three years, the Senators missed the playoffs. Chris scored six goals, had ten assists, and served 210 minutes in the penalty box.

In February, Bryan Murray and the management of the Senators decided that the team needed changes. As a result, a number of players were traded. One of the players who was traded was Mike Fisher. The trio of Alfredsson, Fisher, and Neil—the three great community ambassadors of the team—had one less member.

During the previous summer, Mike had married Carrie Underwood, one of the most famous country music singers out of Nashville who had shot into the limelight when she won the *American Idol* contest. It was necessary for Carrie to be in Nashville, and Mr. Murray knew this. As a result, when he was making changes to the team, he knew in his heart that he should trade Mike to Nashville. The value that Mike was and had been to the team and community was not nearly as important as helping Mike and Carrie have a very successful Christian marriage.

Mike had been the honorary chair of Roger's House, serving in the capacity as the representative of the Senators team and for its off-ice organization, Sports and Entertainment. Roger's House had opened in 2005 beside the Children's Hospital of Eastern Ontario in Ottawa. It's a palliative care home for small children who have severe health problems, especially cancer. It was named after Roger Neilson, the long-time coach in the NHL who finished his time in the NHL as part of the Ottawa Senators management. Roger died of cancer.

As Mike was now leaving Ottawa, a new honorary chair was needed. Fisher recommended his long-time friend, Chris, and Chris's wife,

Cait, to be the new co-chairs. Mike knew that although Chris's reputation on the ice was that of a tough, rugged player, Chris possessed a really big heart. During the years of Chris and Cait's marriage, Fisher had come to realize the importance in Christopher's life of Cait. The two complemented each other.

Chris was already very familiar with Roger's House, as he had visited it a number of times with Mike. Chris understood that the most difficult part of the position was saying goodbye to one of the small patients. The picture of Mike skating on the Senators' ice with a small boy, and then the picture a short time later of Mike carrying the little boy's body in his coffin, was etched in many people's minds, including Chris and Cait's.

As a young boy, Chris received preparation for this position when his mother, Bonnie, took Chris to visit her special needs brother, Ed, in his special home in Owen Sound. Chris was also with his mother when she went to visit her good friend, Florence Richards, when she was in the late stages of MS.

34
The Beginning of the MacLean Era

THE FALL OF 2011 WAS THE BEGINNING OF A NEW ERA IN OTTAWA. PAUL MacLean was the new coach. He had been an assistant to Mr. Babcock in Anaheim, and Babcock had taken him to Detroit when he became the head coach. Paul was an assistant when the Red Wings won the Stanley Cup. He had also worked with Bryan Murray when Bryan was in Anaheim. As a result of coaching in Detroit, MacLean was very aware of the Red Wings' power play system. There usually was a player in front of net to cause problems for the defensive team.

Chris Neil would once again appear on many of the Ottawa power plays. This Ottawa team was not as good as the team that went to the Stanley Cup finals. In fact, the 2011–2012 team was considered to be a rebuilding squad. The rebuilding squad made the playoffs. Paul MacLean was nominated for the Jack Adams Coach of the Year Award. Neil scored thirteen goals, recorded fifteen assists, and added to his team record of penalty minutes with an additional 178 minutes. The NHL all-star game was hosted in Ottawa, with Alfredsson named the captain of one of the teams. In all, five Senators played in the game.

Having finished eighth in their division, Ottawa faced the first place New York Rangers. The series went seven games. Goaltender Craig Anderson allowed an average of two goals per game. In the first game played in New York, Neil scored the winning goal in the second minute of overtime. This goal just added to the intensity of the feelings of the Rangers fans for Neil. There was no question that he was enemy number one.

The author of the book and his wife were travelling home from Arizona when the seventh game of the series was to be played in New York that evening. The Peggs listened to the NHL network on the radio with great interest and enjoyment as the hosts of the show, as well as the call-ins, stated how much Chris, the antagonizer, was disliked in New York. The callers were very adamant that this player was more responsible than anyone else for the series going to the seventh game. Many of the fans believed that Chris, the antagonizer, needed to be neutralized if the Rangers were to win the game.

Captain Alfredsson, along with Jason Spezza, had been benched by MacLean in the third period of game 6 in Ottawa because their efforts were not living up to MacLean's expectations. At the conclusion of game seven, the coach stated that Alfredsson was Ottawa's best player. Alfredsson's efforts were not enough as New York won game seven on home ice after having trailed in the series three games to two. Neil's effort in the game did not go unnoticed. As usual, he gave his best, but the division's top team was just too much.

35
A Short Season

CONTRACT NEGOTIATIONS BETWEEN THE PLAYERS AND THE NHL ONCE AGAIN reared its ugly head. The dispute was not settled until early in 2013, which resulted in a forty-eight-game schedule. Chris didn't see quite as much power play time as he'd been given the previous year. He ended up in this shortened season with four goals and eight assists. He added to his team-record penalty minutes with another 144 minutes in the sin bin.

The Senators finished seventh in their playoff division. After defeating the second place Montreal Canadiens four games to one, they lost in the second round to the first place Pittsburgh Penguins four games to one. Neil picked up four assists.

Coach Paul MacLean went one step further in the coach of the year balloting. After being nominated the previous season, this shortened season found MacLean to be the winner of the Jack Adams Coach of the Year Award. Daniel Alfredsson was the winner of the Mark Messier leadership award.

During the years since their daughter was born, Chris and Cait's family had been blest by the arrival of Cole and Finn. All three children quickly developed a love of ice sports—Hailey in figure skating, and the two boys in hockey.

IN THE SUMMER OF 2013, THE SENATOR NATION WAS DEVASTATED WHEN THE management and their captain didn't reach an agreement on a new contract. From the various stories out of the two camps, it was the other camp that was mainly responsible. In the end, Alfie signed a two-year contract with the Detroit Red Wings, where there were a number of players established on the Red Wings team who came from Alfie's homeland. It also appeared that the Red Wings had a much better shot at winning the Stanley Cup than did Ottawa.

Jason Spezza was named the new captain. There were a number of avid Senators followers who sincerely believed that Christopher Neil should be the new captain, but Spezza had been an assistant captain the previous year. When Spezza was named captain, Neil became an assistant captain alongside the longest-serving Senator at that time, defenseman Chris Phillips.

This was the season that Ottawa's tough man scored his one hundredth goal. It was the season when the NHL remodelled the division structure, and Ottawa became a member of the Atlantic grouping. On March 2, Ottawa had the opportunity of playing in the Heritage Game in Vancouver against the Canucks.

When Alfie came to town with the Red Wings, over twenty thousand fans jammed the arena. The only crowd that was larger in Ottawa was a game with Toronto, which drew about five hundred more fans than the Detroit game. As is usual for a Toronto game in Ottawa, it appeared that the majority of the fans were there for the Leafs.

As the year moved along, the Senators' season became more and more frustrating. Coach MacLean appeared to change his coaching methods and systems. He wasn't coaching with the confidence he had shown in his first couple of seasons. Spezza was not Alfredsson. He showed very little interest in community happenings. He was not respected in the dressing room like Alfie.

The three great community team players—Fisher, Alfie, and Chris Neil—had become one. Chris was still Chris. There was no question that he was always giving a hundred per cent. There was little question that he had to become the leader in the dressing room. On the ice, his line wasn't receiving the same opportunities to dump the puck in and chase it. Chris still was a league leader in hits. He often played with Zack Smith, whose style did complement Neil's, but the line wasn't given the same opportunity to get out on the ice for the purpose of changing the flow of the game to Ottawa's advantage.

Bryan Murray's contract was extended another two years. At the end of the two years, he would become an advisor to the team. His responsibility increased when he was named president of hockey operations. The Senators did not make it to the playoffs.

As the season came to a close, the attendance at the games was often in the seventeen thousand range. There were signs of the community losing interest in their Senators.

37

A Season of Injuries—The Season of "Hamburglar"

THE SEASON OF 2014–2015 WAS THE SEASON CHRIS PLAYED IN ONLY thirty-eight games. That year he fractured his thumb in a fight with Luke Gazdic. This injury ended his regular season.

The season had many ups and downs for the Senators. A positive was that Eric Karlson completely recovered from the major foot injury that had resulted from his entanglement with Matt Cooke, a notorious Pittsburgh player who had received a number of earlier suspensions from the NHL for his conduct on the ice. The league decided that there was no suspension warranted on this contact. The Senators didn't feel this way. Chris Neil took after Cooke as a response to his action against Karlson, a fellow teammate. Chris didn't go after Cooke in such a way as to hurt his team's efforts to win, but in such a manner that everyone knew that Neil would not stand by when one of his fellow players was attacked.

Although Karlson was playing well, the Senators were only playing .500 hockey in mid-December. Bryan Murray decided that there was a need for a coaching change. Paul MacLean was fired. He was replaced by his assistant coach, Dave Cameron. When the month of February rolled around, Ottawa was fourteen points out of a playoff position. Their two regular goaltenders had major injury problems. Andrew Hammond was called up from Binghampton. The Hamburglar, as he was nicknamed, played the best hockey of his career. Ottawa clinched a playoff spot in the last regular season game. The team had set a new NHL record for a comeback after February 1.

The trade deadline was approaching in late February, and a number of teams were showing interest in acquiring Chris. Chris did not wish to leave Ottawa. It was the Chris Neil family home. It was also during this time that Chris hurt his thumb. There was no longer any question. He would be staying in Ottawa.

The attendance in Ottawa was down slightly but was still an average of over eighteen thousand, which was just over ninety-five per cent capacity. Bryan Murray had been diagnosed with cancer during the summer before the season, and he was receiving weekly treatment. Alfie returned home. He signed a one game contract so that he could retire as an Ottawa Senator. It was also the year that the Senators reached the level of having given $100 million to various charitable needs of Western Quebec and Eastern Ontario. Chris was a major reason why this happened.

When the playoffs began with Montreal, Neil was ready to play. However, Cameron was in no hurry to dress Chris, who was a proven playoff performer. After the Senators lost the first two games in Montreal, Christopher was dressed for game three at home. Ottawa eventually lost the series in six games after having won the third game. Neil only played in one other game.

CHRIS WITH ROB REED AND HIS SON BRYANT

CHRIS WITH KELLIE AND ROB REED AT DAN NEIL'S BALL TOURNAMENT

38
Neil Is Ready to Go!

DURING THE SUMMER BEFORE THE 2015 SEASON BEGAN, CHRIS WORKED harder than ever to be in shape. The league was changing. He needed to be faster and lighter. He began training camp having achieved his goals. He looked great.

It soon became apparent that Dave Cameron was not a great Neil fan. Was it possible that Cameron had influenced Paul MacLean, as Chris's role with Ottawa changed during Paul's last season and a half as coach? Is it possible that Cameron had been a big influence in the changes to MacLean's coaching philosophy that led to Paul being fired? It's definitely true that the success of the Senators at the end of the previous season had more to do with Andrew Hammond's unbelievable season in goal than it did with Cameron's leadership.

Chris played most of the season on the team's fourth line. His average ice time per game declined. The fourth line was seldom put on the ice to try and change the pace of the game. It was unusual for Chris to play on the power play. A positive for the team was that Alfie became part of the organization. He was hired as an advisor to hockey operations.

In a silent auction held in the Ottawa area, one of Chris's autographed sticks went for $4,000. During the season, Neil played his nine hundredth game as a Senator. Bryan Murray was retiring at the end of the season. In late February, he signed Christopher to a one-year extension to his contract for a million and a half dollars.

The gradual decline of attendance at Ottawa's games continued. There were games in the last half of the season in which the attendance at a game was just over seventeen thousand fans. There was also a continuing decline of the Senators' involvement in community activity, especially by the players. The Senators missed the playoffs for the second time in three years.

39
The Beginning of the Dorion Era

BRYAN MURRAY RETIRED AS SOON AS THE SEASON ENDED. HIS ASSISTANT, PIERRE Dorion, became the new general manager. His first actions were to fire Cameron and most of his coaching staff. He then hired Guy Boucher, who had previously coached in Tampa. He had been fired in Tampa after a year and a half, even though the team was playing over .500 hockey. It seemed that the Tampa management were not happy with his kitty-bar-the-door style of hockey. After Boucher was hired, it looked as if Chris was going to have a coach who appreciated his style of play. The two had a couple of positive meetings. Mr. Boucher and his family were attending the same church as the Neils.

When training camp began, Neil was in top shape. He looked faster than ever and was very keen to play as he entered the season where he would play his one thousandth game as a Senator. It did not take long into the season, however, for Christopher to discover that Boucher did not think that Chris could play the coach's defensive style game. The coach never gave him much chance to find out. Boucher did not play Chris very much. When he was playing, it was on the fourth line, in which Boucher had little faith. On numerous occasions, Chris played with a couple of players with limited experience who did not play Chris's style of getting the puck deep in the other end, chasing it, and hitting the other team players deep to help change the momentum of the game.

This created no problem for the coach, whose concern was keeping the puck out of the Ottawa goal. This system was very successful, as Ottawa set a new team record at one stage in the season when they went twelve games in a row and never had more than two goals scored against them. The outstanding work of Anderson and his backup, Condon, resulted in the system being successful.

The strength of Chris Neil always had been his forechecking and his play in the offensive end. When Chris was given the rare opportunity to play on the second and third line, Neil looked very much at home. He skated and played at the level of his line mates. As Chris wasn't playing many minutes, his value as an inspirational player for the team declined.

Chris never was a penalty killer. It seemed that Boucher only wanted players with the mindset of a penalty killer, or very close to that mindset. When Chris spoke to Boucher of the possibility of playing sometimes on the power play, the coach replied that the power play was on a different path. The path did not include Neil.

In the meantime, the attendance at Senators games was down considerably. There were those who were stating that the arena's location, which is far from ideal, was the reason. The arena had not moved from the location that had sell out after sell out and was once full of excitement. The team had missed the playoffs two of the last three years. Defensive style hockey does not excite the fans. Was this a major reason that Boucher had been fired in Tampa, even though his team was winning?

Then there was the fact that the trio of Neil, Alfredsson, and Fisher weren't leading the team's involvement in the community. Roger's House, with the Neils as the honorary chair people, was still very significant. But where were the Senator players at other community events? The new players weren't connecting with the people of Ottawa. They weren't involved with young hockey fans as they'd been in past years.

In reality, the Senators weren't impacting the community as they once had when Fisher, Alfredsson, and Neil were very familiar faces. The thousands who loved and appreciated Chris Neil weren't interested in coming to the games to watch their hero sit on the end of the bench.

Letters from Ron

Chris Neil has twenty-seven more games to play for the Ottawa Senators to reach the mark of playing "one thousand" games in a Senators' uniform. Chris, as long as he stays healthy, will reach this goal sometime in December in the upcoming season.

A couple of weeks ago, we wrote about Mike Fisher playing in his one thousandth game. Mike is one of just over 250 players in the history of the NHL to achieve this record. When Chris plays his one thousandth game for the Ottawa Senators, he will become one of less than sixty players in the history of the NHL to play this number of games for one team. Wow!

It will be an amazing achievement for the little freckle-faced, redhead kid from Flesherton who is the son of Barry and the late Bonnie Neil.

Each and every one of us in this area can feel pride in this youngest of four brothers who grew up having to defend himself from his rough and tumble older brothers.

The amazing this about Christopher—his mother always called him that—is that his natural nature is not that of a fighter, although he would not shy away from a fight.

As a small boy, his heart was set on playing in the NHL. He got there in the first place because he was willing to play the role of the tough guy. He easily has the record in Ottawa for the most penalized player in franchise history.

However, the truth of the matter is that he arrived as a fighter but a hockey player broke out. Chris has become an excellent hockey player, with the ability to throw clean hits as well as anyone in the NHL. He can make an excellent pass to another player. Very few in the NHL are as tough in front of the net in screening the goalie as this Flesherton native. When given the opportunity, Christopher also has the ability to score goals.

His true value to the Senators goes much deeper than all of the above. He has shown time and time again that he is the leader in team spirit. He inspires and leads the other players. This has resulted in Christopher being an extremely popular person in the city of Ottawa. More than one person has said that if he ran for mayor of Ottawa, he would win.

This popularity is raised to a higher level with his off-ice activity. The off the ice activity is highlighted by the role that he and his wife, Cait, play in Roger's House, the home that houses many little children who are dying of cancer.

Both Chris and Cait have a great compassion for people. This, of course, can also be seen as they raise their three children, Hailey, Cole, and Finn.

"One Thousand Games," here we come!

---

7   As appeared in *The Flesherton Advance, Dundalk Herald*—September 2016

40
Game One Thousand

For Chris and Cait, the big thing was not the season, although it was important to them. The big event was game one thousand. At the very heart of Chris's NHL career was the desire to play his entire career in Ottawa. Yes, it was and is home. The small-town boy's loyalty was always very evident.

When the season began, game one thousand was scheduled to be played in San Jose. Cathy Pegg had long stated that she was going to the game regardless of where it was played. Ron and Cathy had their plane tickets scheduled for San Jose in early December.

Chris missed one game. As a result, the big game was to happen in Los Angeles. This was great for the Pegg family, who live many miles apart. Rob, the second son, and his family live in the area. James, his older brother, would fly in from Saskatchewan with his two oldest children. One of these boys, Kaden, is a very avid Ottawa fan. Chris's little chum from his early life, Stacey, would fly in from Dallas with her two girls. A Pegg family reunion would be part of Chris's one thousandth game. Cait flew from Ottawa.

For most people—family, friends, and fans—it wasn't practical to go to LA. The Senators organization realized this. The celebration of the big game would take place in Ottawa upon the team's return a few days later.

Because it was his big game, the coach placed Chris in the opening lineup. At the appropriate time in the game, the PA announcer took time to pay tribute to Chris, and the fans responded with a big round of applause.

Chris played a typical Chris game. He played a few minutes more than usual.

Letters from Ron

Chris Neil was a twelve-year-old playing Peewee hockey in Flesherton. I was the team's coach.

At Christmas time, the Peggs and Neils always shared a meal celebrating the season. On the evening we were celebrating when Chris was a Peewee hockey player, we also had a hockey practice.

It was necessary for Chris and me to leave the celebration and go to the arena. As we were leaving, one of Chris's older brothers asked the question of Chris: "Who is your coach?"

Without hesitation, Chris responded, "My Mother." Most of us laughed, including me. Chris's response was not a surprise to any of us.

His mother is a very major reason for Chris achieving his goal of playing one thousand games in the NHL with one team, and on top of that he is only the fifty-third player in the entire history of the NHL to play one thousand games with one team.

As he was playing that one thousandth game in Los Angeles, a number of us had numerous thoughts of Bonnie as the game was played. Talking with Chris after the game, he stated that he too had many thoughts of his mother during the game.

At one point in the game he received a penalty for slashing, which appeared to be completely a wrong call. Chris talked quietly to the officials who were in front of the penalty box. He then went into the box. The officials kept talking. They then waved Chris out of the box. Their discussion had led them to reverse the call. My wife said that it was probably Bonnie up in heaven who really got the penalty reversed.

In the process of this game I was continuously impressed by that which we already knew. Chris is much more than a fighter. He made at least two perfect passes to teammates, who then had excellent shots on goal.

In a game that the other team had already won, Chris body checked one of their players with a textbook body hit. There was less than two minutes left in the game, but Chris was doing what he always has done in

Ottawa. He was giving his best to the very end. He was showing by example what needed to be done.

That is why on December 14 it was Chris Neil Day in Ottawa.

Thank you, Chris, and thank you, Bonnie. And by the way, thanks to Cait, who has continuously carried on the work in Chris's life that was begun by his mother.[8]

---

8   As appeared in *The Dundalk Herald, Flesherton Advance*—December 2016

CATHY PEGG WITH CHRIS

RON AND CATHY PEGG WITH CHRIS AND CAIT

PEGG FAMILY WITH CHRIS AND CAIT

PEGG BOYS WITH CHRIS

Letters from Ron

Trenton is one of our two family members who was born with special needs. Trent, as we know him, was born nine years ago last December.

His mom and dad, Angela and Rob, found out from the doctors that he was not going to be a normal child. He had problems from his very beginnings. There was absolutely no question that Angela would give birth to his special needs child. This was not a matter for discussion.

In the last days before Trent was to be born, a further problem developed. Angela could not hear Trent in her womb. She called the doctor, who told her to get to the hospital immediately.

Trent was immediately removed from the womb. It was discovered that the nasty cord, which is so important in birth, had caught around his neck. If he had not been delivered, he would have died in a few hours. Some of the doctors were not encouraging to the parents. At least one doctor told them that Trent would be nothing more than a vegetable.

The following months and years were a major struggle for the new baby and his parents. From the start, his mother, Angela, was amazing. She would not take no for an answer. She got for Trent all of the help that was available. The little guy had operation after operation. There were many medical specialists in Colorado who helped Trent in a variety of ways. Angela once said to my wife, "Don't ever think of Trent as a burden. He is a great big labour of love."

By the time he was five he still could not walk without help. He was considered legally blind, but by holding his head a certain way this young child could see. There was a blind school that he could go to, which would be helpful in many ways.

We went to see him at the school. He was a leader for his classmates as he flew around the building with his walker. I was just at the stage that I was going to need some help walking around. When I saw Trent flying around with his walker, he was an inspiration to me. If the walker could do this for our little guy, then it could help me. It was not *long after this that we purchased my first walker. Today, Trent can fly around without a walker. My walker is a major blessing for me.*

When we were recently at Chris Neil's 1,000th game in LA, Trent was there. I did not have my walker. The arena provided me with a wheelchair. When the game was over and I was sitting in the chair waiting for my helper to arrive, I suddenly was moving. Trent was pushing me as his face shone with his usual smile.

To God be the Glory.[9]

41
The Celebration

THE FLOODGATES OPENED. ALL ROADS FROM FLESHERTON AND GREY COUNTY led to Ottawa for the celebration. It was Chris Neil Day in Ottawa. The city had designated the day as Chris's day. Hundreds of fans from the Flesherton area were at the game. A number of these were former Grey County people who now lived in the Ottawa area. It was a magnificent celebration that can be best described by the following pictures.

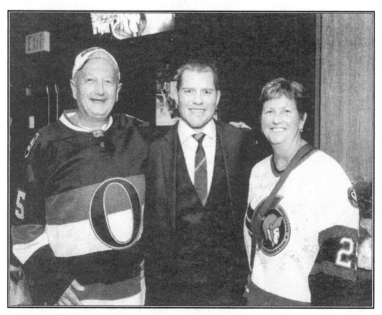

CHRIS WITH CATHY AND FRANK COLTON

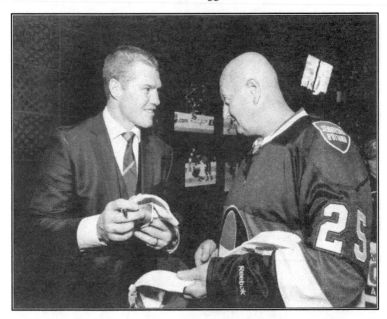

CHRIS WITH FRANK COLTON

CHRIS WITH KEN AND GLENDA RICHARDSON

CHRIS WITH CAM AND MARY RICHARDSON

PHOTO INCLUDES BARRY NEIL (CHRIS'S DAD), LARRY MILLER, MP,
JIM DAVIS, AND NANCY EVANS

42
The End—Or is it?

IT WAS ONLY A SHORT TIME AFTER THIS GAME THAT BOUCHER INFORMED CHRIS that he would not be receiving much ice time in the future. He became a healthy scratch for a number of games. This was a new experience. When he was dressed, he continued to play with a couple of very inexperienced players. These players changed from game to game. Neil's ice time was very limited. Ottawa continued to win. The crowds at the games continued to diminish. Chris suffered a finger injury in late February.

Ottawa was in the playoffs. In their series against New York, the team was not playing well. They showed very little spirit and even less backbone. One of New York's physical players was hitting the Senators' players with no counter response by the Ottawa team. The coach decided to dress Chris. It was not long into the game before the New York player was at it again, but Neil was on the ice. Typically, Neil went after this New York "tough" guy. Neil pounded him. Chris had the fans on their feet cheering. His fellow players were congratulating him. The Senators had new life. His total ice time for the game was less than three minutes, but there was no question that Christopher Neil was the star of the game.

The fans gave him a continuous standing ovation. A member of his teammates stated that Neil was the star of the game. Chris was not only the star of the game—he was the star of the series. The Senators came roaring back to win. With Neil's leadership in his brief appearance, a much more physical Ottawa team and a more exciting team emerged.

Neil only played in one more game, and that was only briefly. He had broken a finger in his exchange with the Ranger opponent.

There is, however, little question that Christopher Neil's leadership was an important factor in Ottawa taking the Pittsburgh Penguins into overtime in game seven in the Stanley Cup eastern finals. In spite of not dressing and not playing in games, he had continued to be a positive influence in the dressing room with the other players on his team. In other words, he continued to be Chris Neil.

The season was over. Chris and the Senators talked about a new contract, but Chris did not want to return to Ottawa with the possibility of attempting to play for Coach Boucher. The coach did not want him back. The end result was that there was a mutual agreement that the team and Chris would not be involved in contract negotiations. Chris was a free agent.

Over the course of the summer, Neil did receive concrete offers from other teams. At least one offer was for a substantial amount of money. Chris wasn't sure … or was he? It seemed that the only offer he might consider would be one from Montreal. He was also aware that he had suffered a number of hand injuries during the recent seasons. Was he actually willing to play any other place that Ottawa? The final answer was that he retired in December 2017.

His retirement was announced at a news conference. He was retiring as a Senator. The news conference was on television and Facebook. The Facebook website has been visited by over 110,000 people. Meanwhile, the Senators have struggled on the ice and off. The number of fans continues to decline, and as the Senators aren't getting great goaltending, the team is not presently in playoff contention.

The Senators no longer have Alfie, who quit his executive position early in the 2017–2018 season—no Fisher, no Neil, and Bryan Murray has joined Chris's mother. Then comes the big concluding question: Who have the Senators replaced these icons with?

Somebody said that it couldn't be done,
But he with a chuckle replied
That he would be one
Who wouldn't say so.

So he buckled right in;
If he worried, he hid it.
He started to skate
As he tackled the thing
That couldn't be done, and he did it.

Letters from Ron

A number of us became interested in the Ottawa Senators when Chris Neil became a member of that team. There were quite a few of us who became fans. We had never thought of cheering for this team before that time. When they reached the Stanley Cup finals against Anaheim, the amount of local excitement reached a new high.

When Chris began playing for this team, the management of the Senators was very concerned that the team should be involved with the community in the Ottawa area. The players were asked with which charity did they want to be involved. Players like Chris, Mike Fisher, and Daniel Alfredsson became well known for their community efforts. Mike Fisher often came to Flesherton with Chris and became a very high profile person in this community as he joined Chris in giving to this area.

When Bonnie Neil was killed in a single vehicle car accident just over twelve years ago, there were eight members of the Senator organization—players and management—who flew to Owen Sound to attend her funeral.

Chris's playing days are now over. The Senators no longer have a high community profile. Players are no longer asked what charity they would like to work with. The question today is: Would you be willing to work with a charity? If there is a question even asked.

This 2017–2018 season has seen the Senators close down over two thousand seats in the arena. Even with their seats closed for use, the Senators aren't selling out the arena. The argument of some is that the arena isn't in a good location. It's not easy to reach and, as a result, it takes time to get to the arena. This is true, but it didn't used to be a problem.

When you are going to visit someone you care about, the location factor is not a problem. However, if it is a casual relationship, the location can become an excuse.

Mike Fisher was traded to Nashville by Bryan Murray so that he would be in the same city as his wife, whose singing career demanded that she be in Nashville. Brian Murray cared about his people. Since last season, Brian has joined Bonnie Neil. Daniel Alfredsson has left the Ottawa organization. Chris Neil has retired. When the coach allowed Chris to make some brief appearances in a game in the playoffs, Chris was greeted by thunderous applause and standing ovations. Most observers agree that his leadership was responsible for awakening the Senators, leading them to win the series and even reach the Stanley Cup semifinals before losing out to the eventual Stanley Cup champions, Pittsburgh, in the seventh game of the series in overtime.

Yes, that community involvement was still there last year, although not as noticeable.

This year it does not appear to be present.[10]

---

10 As appeared in *The Flesherton Advance, Dundalk Herald*–January 2018

Bonus Trivia

"He shoots, he scores" (Foster Hewitt)

WHEN CATHY COLTON OF FLESHERTON EMAILED A NUMBER OF THE PICTURES which are in this book, she wrote the following: "We are so happy that you are writing the book. We [she and Frank] have so enjoyed watching Chris, and he has made us very proud! He is a very popular guy, and somehow I believe that the best might be yet to come for Chris. He can use the power of his influence to really make differences in whatever he chooses to do next."

On one occasion when Chris was in public school in Flesherton, the school maintenance people had put in a new pad of cement just outside the gym entrance. The maintenance people had put up a large sign to remind people not to use this door. The young redhead either didn't see the sign or chose to ignore it. He went out the door and walked across the pad, leaving his prints behind him. The new pad of cement had to be replaced.

Bob and Ruth Butler, along with Ron and Cathy Pegg, were holidaying at the timeshare resort at Calabogie. It is on the same lake as the Neil's summer home. The four went to visit. Just as they were getting ready to leave, the women wanted some pictures. The mantle in front of the fireplace looked like a good place. It was not difficult for Ron to get down to sit on the mantle. It was not so easy when he wanted to get up. Chris decided that he would pull the old guy up. He pulled straight out. He slipped. He ended up on the floor with Ron on top of him. No harm was done, but wouldn't it have made a great story if Chris had been hurt? "Senators tough guy injured while trying to help senior citizen to his feet."

Saturday, June 23, 2018, is going to be "Chris Neil Appreciation Day" in Flesherton and Grey Highlands.

In mid-April 2018, Chris returned to the Senators when he signed a contract to be Alumni Ambassador.

Go Senators Go!

Bibliography

Goodreads. "Walter D. Wintle, Quotes." Accessed April 4, 2018. https://www.goodreads.com/quotes/1033193-if-you-think-you-are-beaten-you-are-if-you.

Del Mundo, Rob. *Hockey's Enforcers—A Dying Breed*. Toronto: Moydart Press, 2016.

Pegg, Ron. "Letters from Ron." *Dundalk Herald/Flesherton Advance,* May, 2016.

Charuk, Dan. "Senator Practices with Hanover Team," *The Hanover Post*, February 19, 2002.

Zwolinski, Mark. "Neil Among the Best of Pests," *Toronto Star*, May 6, 2002.

Jackson, Johnathon. "Neil Frustrated Over Senators' Loss," *Owen Sound Sun Times*, May 15, 2002.

Pegg, Ron. "Letters from Ron." *Dundalk Herald/Flesherton Advance,* September, 2016.

Ibid. December, 2016.

Pegg, Ron. "Letters from Ron." *Flesherton Advance*, January, 2017.

Pegg, Ron. "Letters from Ron." *Dundalk Herald/Flesherton Advance*, January, 2018.

Also by Ron Pegg

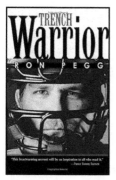

Trench Warrior
978-0884197805
Creation Books, 2001

It is said that one person can make a difference...but have you ever wondered if your life really counts? This testimony of one man's fight, his refusal to let his adversary overtake him and his trust in the orders of his Commanding Officer, will inspire and challenge you to let God use your life to accomplish great things for Him.

The Last of the Small Town Boys
978-1553069539
Essence Publishing, 2005

The rural village of southern Ontario where each person knew every other person, as well as each person's family history for at least three generations past, represents an era of history. Like *Anne of Green Gables*, *Tom Sawyer*, and *Sunshine Sketches of a Little Town* represent a time that is no more, *The Last of the Small-Town Boys* celebrates the passing of another time.

Cow Pasture Beginnings
978-1554520497
Essence Publishing, 2006

John McGraw, in 1913, stated: "Naturally, I think baseball is the most admirable pastime in the world, a keen combination of wit, intelligence and muscle. It develops the mind, establishes discipline and gives to those who take part in it sound bodies, clear heads and a better sense of life" (*The Old Ball Game*, Frank Deford).

They Call Him Garney, I Call Him Dad
978-1-926676-12-8
Word Alive Press, 2009

Garney Pegg was the owner of a small town bakery and grocery in Beeton, Ontario for almost thirty years. The business began in the first year of the Great Depression and carried on through World War II and the 1950's. He and his wife Pearl raised a family of five while facing all of the problems that a small business faced in the hazardous time of the Depression and the War.

Giant Among Giants: Ernest C. Manning
978-1-926676-82-1
Word Alive Press, 2010

"After sixty years of having studied Ernest C. Manning and following his career, I firmly believe that the man who was elected in seven consecutive elections as Premier of Alberta, and who never faced a close election in his entire political career, a man who still can be heard on repeat broadcasts of Canada's National Bible Broadcast, is one of Canada's greatest people."

–Ron Pegg

Servant of the Shepherd King
978-1-77069-557-3
Word Alive Press, 2012

Can one servant make a difference?

"Ron Pegg has been a beacon of light for his family, friends, school, neighbors, church, various sorts and community. His love for God is obvious, and his love for humankind is expressed in his mission to the community and beyond. He has been a support and mentor to many people, including myself. You will enjoy reading about the life story of a man totally committed to his Lord and Savior."

–Marin Garniss
Providence, Manitoulin Island, Ontario
The Peggs' pastor

Tribute
978-1-77069-585-6
Word Alive Press, 2012

To God be the Glory! It was in the late 1970s when the Walls family and Frank Macintyre of the Dundalk Herald gave Ron Pegg the opportunity of writing a weekly column for the Flesherton Advance. During the next three decades he wrote the column under a number of different names. This book includes articles from that column, along with many recent works.

Here's Mrs. A: Canada's Woman of the 21st Century
978-1-4866-0500-2
Word Alive Press, 2014

Kate Aiken's young life experiences in Beeton were of the utmost importance in molding her into Canada's beloved "Mrs. A". Dubbed by her CFRB co-host Gordon Sinclair as the busiest woman in the world, she was a feminine dynamo who shared each of her experiences with her audience who loved her for what she was.

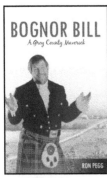

Bognor Bill: A Grey County Maverick
978-1-4866-1316-8
Word Alive Press, 2016

"I knew I wanted a front-row seat on [Bill's] re-election campaign in 2003. The man was a local legend, and my journalistic curiosity naturally drove me to question how much of it was myth. To the outsiders, the riding of Bruce-Grey-Owen Sound was at times insignificant, but the Bognor native who represented it was not."

"The only time I've seen MPP Murdoch pause reflectively was when he talked about the hardship, the work ethic, and the pride of his people at home. And that's what he liked to call them: my people. I never doubted he had his people's back. That was one part of his genius. He had Bruce and Grey born and bred in his bones and always had the pulse of his people's needs and wants. The other part of his genius was that he truly listened to the people, albeit he didn't always agree with them."

—Ana Sajfert
Legislative Aide, Queens Park

CPSIA information can be obtained
at www.ICGtesting.com
Printed in the USA
BVHW07080302011 9
536776BV00020B/3954/P